The Comeback Kid

Portrait of Mayor Mowrer which hangs in Bethlehem City Hall, painted by Peter Schnore, 1998

The Comeback Kid

What You Didn't Know about Mayor Mowrer

Gordon B. Mowrer

Gordon B Mowrer

Bethlehem, Pennsylvania

Mike:

Your a great person and have done much for others. Thank you for all you do! Hope you enjoy the book.

Gordy M.

First Edition

ISBN 978-0-615-37448-2

Available from the Moravian Book Shop
    428 Main Street, Bethlehem, PA 18018
    www.moravianbookshop.com

Printed by Chernay Printing, Inc., Coopersburg, PA

To my family:

Mary

George and Betsy
Ruthie and Greg
Margaret

Rick, Katie, Maggie, Nicholas, Forrest,
Kira, Noah, and Jaxson

and to the Future of Bethlehem

Contents

Foreword

I have often thought about keeping a journal to write a book like this one someday. Life does go by pretty fast. I'm glad that Gordon wrote this book. For me it is an inspiration for me to eventually do the same; for many it will be a shared walk down memory lane.

The stories are familiar – from the campaigning to the occasional infighting with council and the challenges in running a city. This book also gives the reader the details of what is perhaps Gordon's most lasting legacy to the city. It was he who stopped the destructive "urban renewal" movement in downtown Bethlehem before it was too late. He helped save enough buildings to maintain the critical mass of history and sense of place. He knew that what made Bethlehem special was its history, and it was upon that foundation that Bethlehem's future would be built.

Most of the accomplishments that I am most proud of as Mayor of the City of Bethlehem are things that people would never know and might in fact be surprised by. As mayors, our proudest moments are not associated with a public announcement or a press event, but rather the quiet times when we abide by our convictions and take a stand for what we believe, the times we made the right call or quietly helped someone in need. You will not know of my proudest moments until I write my memoir, but this book takes you behind the scenes of Gordon's rather interesting life and gives the reader the opportunity to understand important moments in Bethlehem's history and to know Gordon's proudest moments from his own perspective.

If I had a nickel for every time I was asked why Bethlehem has been so successful in reinventing itself and rebounding from the loss of steel, I would be a rich man. I am not sure I know all the reasons, but one of them most certainly is Gordon Mowrer and his contributions to our community. Bethlehem is a special place made even more special by people like Gordon Mowrer.

There are very few people who know what it is like to sit in "the chair" as Mayor of Bethlehem. In addition to Gordon's ability as mayor, businessman and councilman, he also is a pastor who possesses a great ability to put problems into perspective. This is perhaps the quality that I've come to appreciate the most. There have been numerous occasions when I would be frustrated by a particular situation or conflict and I would be discussing this with Gordon. Inevitably, he would put his hand on my shoulder, look straight into my eyes and calmly and reverently say, "This, too, shall pass." And you know what? He was always right, and as much as that was not what I wanted to hear at the moment, it was true.

Gordon has been a trusted mentor and friend. He is able to see things from many points of view. Gordon could always tell when I was having a particularly tough day, whether it was from an early morning phone call or a casual conversation at Rotary. On those days he would invariably stop by unannounced late in the afternoon to chat. The first couple of times I thought it was by chance, but Gordon had a way with people, and could tell when I needed a sounding board to vent. I will always be grateful to him for this guidance, and I hope to be in a position someday in my life to return the favor to a future mayor.

We all wish that sometimes we could go back and change certain things that we have done. The old saying,

"If I only knew then what I know now," applies to all of us at some point in our lives. I get the sense sometimes that Gordon would do some things differently as mayor had he had the wisdom and expertise that he has today. I think in some respects we have formed a strong bond between us, not only because of our common experiences as Mayor of Bethlehem, but also perhaps it has been an opportunity for Gordon to share his thoughts on things he might have done differently and impart his wisdom to me. Gordon sees some of himself in me, and rather than hold back, he has unselfishly tried to help me overcome potential pitfalls. For that I will always be grateful.

Gordon has, on his latest tour of duty in City Hall, worked quietly behind the scenes as a leader and consensus builder. He has always had the right motivation and intentions, and as a result has earned the trust of many. In the end, it is all about making a difference and leaving your community better than before you started. Gordon has clearly accomplished this feat.

So, whether you are a Bethlehem history buff or a budding local politician, sit back, get comfortable, and enjoy the book.

John Callahan
Mayor of Bethlehem

Acknowledgments

Writing a book takes a lot of help from a lot of people. Special thanks go to Susan M. Dreydoppel, local historian and editor, for the many talents she brought to putting this book together: transcribing and typing, editing, researching, preparing the manuscript for publication, and the other tasks which she performed so professionally.

My thanks for memories, discussion, encouragement and support, fact-checking, and a multitude of other gifts great and small go to:

Jeff Andrews
Ismael Arcelay
Glenn Asquith
John Callahan
Dolores Caskey
David Diehl
Harry Fisher
Dan Fitzpatrick
Carol Dean Henn
Eric Herrenkohl
Ray Holton
Pat Kesling

Russ "Larry" Laros
Jim McCarthy
Anne McGeady
Jeff Parks
Bob Rudas
Joan Schrei
Vangie Sweitzer
Barbara Martin Stout
Bucky Szulborski
Joseph Trilli
Stanley Zweifel
Dotty Zug

Chernay Printing, Inc., especially Rick Knapp, Chris Severn and Dave Henry

The Moravian Book Shop, especially Dana DeVito and

The Mowrers: Mary, George, Ruthie Mowrer Huron, Margaret Mowrer Sharpe, Betsy, Rick, Nick, my brother Tip and his wife Barbara

Credits

Some of the photographs in this book are from my personal collection, some are from official scrapbooks kept during my years as mayor, and some are from local newspapers. All photographs from the *Morning Call* and the *Bethlehem Globe-Times* are reprinted with permission of the *Morning Call* or the *Express-Times*, the successor newspaper to the *Bethlehem Globe-Times*.

WGPA radio programs which are quoted in this book come from an audiotape of selected programs which were aired in 1976. The tape is in my personal collection, and it was transcribed so it could be used in this book.

He Left his Mark on Bethlehem

"Gordon Mowrer's accomplishments have left their mark on Bethlehem."
Morning Call Editorial, December 22, 1977

The downtown Bethlehem that we know today – Main Street between Church and Broad Streets, with its distinctive specialty shops, animated pedestrians strolling the slate sidewalks or relaxing at outdoor café tables, colorful architectural details and period street lights – would not exist had it not been for Gordon Mowrer.

Gordon Mowrer served as Mayor of Bethlehem two times, elected to one term from 1974 to 1977 and appointed to serve one year in 1987. During each term he initiated and promoted a new vision of Bethlehem's future: preserving what was called the Main Street corridor and highlighting almost 250 years of historic architecture during his first term, and advocating for year-round tourism during his second. The timing was such that each vision fell to his successor to carry out, and to their credit, they followed through.

Ironically, the vision of preserving historic Bethlehem rather than tearing it down and building a "modern" downtown is one of the reasons he served only one elected term. When Mowrer proposed his idea soon after he was elected, it was the exact opposite of the way the city had been moving under Mayor Gordon Payrow. Mowrer's vision mirrored what was becoming a national trend – emphasis on preservation rather than redevelopment – but the trend was still continuing to emerge. Mowrer inherited parts of the old redevelopment plan and conscientiously completed or continued to advance some aspects that were already underway: what was called the First Valley Bank Plaza at Broad and New Streets, the Plaza Mall, and the Walnut Street parking garage. But he and his city planners were attempting to merge that renewal effort on Broad Street with his new vision for preserving Main Street. He faced continuous opposition and obstinacy from the Bethlehem Redevelopment Authority leadership throughout his term, although it played little part in his administration or his plans. During the campaign for his second term as mayor, the head of the Bethlehem Redevelopment Authority, as well as the New York City consultants who developed the original renewal plans, backed Mowrer's opponent. Mowrer lost his bid for a second term in the primary election.

Congressman Fred B. Rooney, who headed Mowrer's unsuccessful campaign for mayor in 1969, told a farewell gathering of Mowrer's friends and supporters at the end of his term in 1977 that "four years . . . was too short to see results."[1] In the case of the downtown, it has taken decades for the results to be appreciated, and the full results still may not be known. Most people who walk down the street think that it has "always" been this way, and do not realize that Bethlehem came close to something very different.

To get an idea of what downtown Bethlehem, and in particular Main Street, might have been, park your car (preferably in the Walnut Street parking garage) and walk to Broad Street. Walk around the office building and bank at the corner of Broad and New Streets, the patch of grass

---

[1]"Friends, Political Foes Honor Outgoing Mayor," Dan Church, *Bethlehem Globe-Times*, November 28, 1977, p. 4.

and fountain, the adjoining office buildings. Look at the new five-story building diagonally across the street, and the older buildings at the other two corners. Walk past the developing "Restaurant Row" to the corner of Broad and Main. Turn around and look back, noticing how the bank plaza building juts into the street, and how the building itself looks out of place with the rest of the street.

Then turn and walk down Main Street, noticing the well-maintained buildings with their period architectural details, the trees which provide a welcoming feel (and which are lighted at night year-round with tiny white lights, giving a magical quality to the street), the outdoor tables and the shops. Compare the number of people you see on the street here with those you saw at the bank plaza.

Had it not been for Gordon Mowrer, Main Street could have looked just like the corner at Broad and New. The historic buildings would have been torn down and replaced with modern high-rise buildings, with several large department stores and a street mall. This is what Bethlehem could have been. This is what Allentown attempted, and ultimately has repudiated. This is what Gordon Mowrer and his administration wanted to prevent.

Then there is his second vision: promoting year-round tourism. Mowrer's idea was to build on the success of Christmas buses and the influx of visitors during Musikfest to make Bethlehem a tourist destination throughout the year. He presented his *Tourism Proposal for the City of Bethlehem* in September, 1987, and spent the remainder of the year promoting it to the public, often showing the video to one civic group at a time.

The proposal, which is printed as an appendix in this book, called for the creation and funding of a separate governmental authority, which Mowrer felt was the best way to develop tourism in Bethlehem. The Bethlehem Tourism Authority was born in 1988; it died in 2001. Yet Mowrer's vision of year-round tourism lives on as a continuing goal. Its intent has been supported through the years by numerous local and downtown business and historical organizations, by Discover Lehigh Valley (formerly the Lehigh Valley Convention and Visitors Bureau; founded in 1984, it was a fledgling organization at the time of Mowrer's original vision), and by the growth and development of the organization now known as ArtsQuest.   It is worth noting that Jeff Parks, the founder and president of ArtsQuest, got his original inspiration for Musikfest from a Bicentennial event held during Gordon Mowrer's first term in office.

Mowrer was thirty-six years old when he was elected to his first term, becoming Bethlehem's youngest mayor to that point.   When he came to City Hall, he brought with him some fresh ideas on dealing with problems. As this is being written, thirty-six years after he first became mayor, and more than two decades after his second term, many of the problems which concerned him as mayor still have a contemporary ring: improving the disposal of trash and solid waste, encouraging the use of bicycles to decrease dependence on gasoline, and other environmental (today called "green") issues; making government services more accessible and responsive to the public (today called "transparency"); declaring City Hall "smoke-free," requiring the use of seat belts, and calling for compassion and common sense in dealing with people with AIDS; bringing computers and technology to the City Hall offices.

Was Mowrer really a prophetic mayor whose ideas were ahead of his time? Whatever your answer to that question, Bethlehem residents and visitors alike should be grateful for his ideas and his vision and for the many programs and actions which they provided. Gordon Mowrer truly has left his mark on Bethlehem.

Susan M. Dreydoppel
Local Historian
January 2010

Chapter

1

In the Beginning

If I had to lose something, like my hearing or my eyesight, what is it I would want least to lose? The thing I would want to lose the least would be my memory, because when you lose your memory, you lose a total sense of history.

Mayor Gordon B. Mowrer, Memorial Day, 1987

People often ask me what it was like to be mayor, and whether I would like to write a book sharing some of the experiences that I had when I was mayor. I have recently spent a lot of time thinking about my earlier years, especially those in politics. This is a book of thoughts and recollections, stories and memories of my political years. The purpose is to write down what I remember, to pass it on to my family and to those who are interested in politics and the history of Bethlehem. My hope is to help them understand my political career and some of the issues I faced. This is one person's view of being mayor, seen through my inner thoughts, personal experiences, and a bit of what went on behind the scenes.

Looking at my family background, there appears to be a family inclination toward politics. In 1918, my grandfather, George A. Brown, became chief burgess of the borough

Borough of Northampton Heights

Ordinance No. 55.

Providing for the annexation of the Borough of Northampton Heights adjoining the City of Bethlehem on the eastern boundary thereof to said City of Bethlehem.

BE IT ORDAINED AND ENACTED BY THE BOROUGH OF NORTHAMPTON HEIGHTS IN TOWN COUNCIL ASSEMBLED, AND IT IS HEREBY ENACTED BY THE AUTHORITY OF THE SAME:

SECTION 1. That more than three-fifths of the taxable inhabitants of the Borough of Northampton Heights having presented petitions asking therefor, the said Borough of Northampton Heights be and the same is hereby annexed to the City of Bethlehem, provided, however, that the Mayor and City Council of the City of Bethlehem shall within a reasonable time after the effective date of this ordinance enact the proper ordinance or ordinances annexing said Borough to said City.

SECTION 2. That a certified copy of this ordinance and the original petitions hereinbefore mentioned shall, immediately after the effective date hereof be presented to the Mayor and City Council of the City of Bethlehem.

SECTION 3. That this ordinance is declared to be urgent and necessary for the immediate preservation of public peace, health and safety, and shall take effect and be in force from and after its passage.

SECTION 4. That all ordinances and parts of ordinances inconsistent herewith be, and the same are, hereby repealed.

Enacted into an ordinance and passed at the Borough of Northampton Heights, this sixteenth day of September, 1918.

FRED. S. MACK,
President of Town Council.

Attest:

HARRY A. BODDER,
Borough Secretary.

Approved this 16th day of September, 1918,

GEORGE A. BROWN,
Chief Burgess.

A copy of this ordinance was found in a wall of the old Saucona Hotel, on Bethlehem's South Side, when it was being demolished. The official ordinance was signed by my grandfather, George A. Brown. *Courtesy the Express-Times*

My grandfather Brown is the man standing in front, wearing civilian clothes. I do not know what the occasion was or why this picture was taken.

of Northampton Heights, located on the south side of the Lehigh River on the eastern border of what had been known as South Bethlehem. He was the chief burgess for only one weekend because the man who was the regular chief burgess had run off with somebody else's wife and was not available to sign an official ordinance. So on September 16, 1918 my grandfather signed "Ordinance #55, providing for the annexation of the Borough of Northampton Heights adjoining the City of Bethlehem on the eastern boundary thereof to said City of Bethlehem." As a result of that ordinance, Northampton Heights became a part of Bethlehem.

On my father's side of the family, my grandfather Mowrer was president of the school board in Spring City and Royersford, Pennsylvania in the early 1900s. My father, Clifton E. Mowrer, Sr., was a member of Bethlehem

City Council from 1964-68. He cast the deciding vote so that the city could borrow the money to finance building the City Center complex, where City Hall and the public library are now. My brother, Clifton "Tip" Mowrer, Jr., served on the Bethlehem School Board from 1968-72, and he also served on the Northampton County Area Community College board (now Northampton Community College). So I have members of two sides of my family who were involved in past civic and government activities. To my knowledge, that is the extent of the political background in my family.

I was never supposed to grow up to become mayor. In fact, I was never supposed to grow up at all. When I was born on February 9, 1936, no one expected me to live. I was very sick and was put in an oxygen tent and given numerous blood transfusions. After a couple of days, the doctor sent my mother, Margaret, home, telling her that she would probably never see me alive again. As my parents left the hospital, my mother said to my father, "I would like to see the baby again before we go home." So the two of them walked out to the area where I was – I was in an incubator behind glass windows – and as my mother and father looked at me, a man and a woman came rushing up to the window, and the woman said, "I want to see the baby that's going to die tonight." I remember my mother telling that story; she said it sent an incredible shock through her system to hear someone say something like that, even though she thought it might happen that way. That was the first time I wasn't supposed to make it, and I did. I came back.

I was born and raised in Bethlehem. My father owned and operated Mowrer's Dairy, located at 1414 Millard Street on the north end of Bethlehem. Milk went in one

The Cup

side of the dairy, and ice cream came out the other side. In 1929 my father opened a small store across the street called The Cup, which sold ice cream cones, sundaes and milkshakes, as well as milk, eggs, cheese, and anything that could be considered a dairy product. The Cup building was designed by my father, and looked like a big milkshake cup, complete with a straw. It became a landmark in the city of Bethlehem. Eventually he opened other Cup stores in other places, ending up with a total of seventeen Cups, and he obtained a patent on the design of the building.

During the course of my growing up years, I think I worked in almost every department in the dairy, beginning when I was quite young. My first job as a little boy was picking up the empty milkshake cups that people had thrown to the ground around The Cup in Bethlehem after they had finished their milkshakes. I would get paid a penny a cup

for picking them up and throwing them away.

When I was really small, I would go to the dairy with my father on Sunday morning, before church. We used to have a big heated tank of soft chocolate, and we would dip vanilla ice cream bars in it. Sometimes I would stick my hands in the chocolate and then lick the chocolate off my fingers. One Sunday I was dressed in a little white suit, and stuck my hands in the chocolate in the tank. When the manager of the department saw me, I quickly wiped my hands on the back of my white pants and coat. Needless to say, my father was not happy with me, and my mother was not happy with my father for not watching me. I was paddled big time!

My father was an Eastern Intercollegiate Champion wrestler for Penn State in 1919, and because of this, my father was always my hero. In fact, when Dad would come home, my brother, Tip, and I would clear the furniture in the living room and put it off to the side, and we would wrestle until something was broken. Then my mother would come in and say, "That's it! No more wrestling!" and we would reluctantly break it up. When you have a father who is an Eastern Intercollegiate Champion, and you like wrestling yourself, and you learned as a little kid how to do some of the basic holds, life becomes slightly different. Wrestling has always been a part of my life.[1]

---

[1] When I became a father, I sent my son, George, to Michael Caruso's wrestling clinic at Allentown College, hoping that he would carry on the family tradition. When my son came home, he said, "I liked everything about the wrestling clinic except the wrestling." He had a great time, but never became a great wrestler.

I have loved ice cream from the time I was a little kid; still do today.

The Mowrer brothers, Tip (Clifton, Jr.) and Gordy.

When I was little, Tip was my idol because he was my older brother. He, of course, never wanted to be bothered with me. But we grew up to be good friends.

The Hamilton Elementary School Orchestra was the first fifth grade orchestra in the Bethlehem School District and, as far as I know, the only orchestra in the district ever to be conducted and put together by a fifth grader.

front, left to right: Richard Achey, accordion; Gordon Mowrer, Ronald Frey, and Paul Kimmel, trumpets; Pasquale "Pat" Zulli and (unknown) Bartholomew, clarinets; Larry Laros, trombone; Floyd Kocher, accordion.

back, left to right: Myron Genel, violin; Harold Feist, drum; David Diehl, conductor; (unknown), drum; (unknown) Walker, violin.

When I began going to school, I attended Penn Elementary School, at the corner of Main and Fairview Streets (where the William Penn Elementary School is now). In fifth grade I moved to Hamilton Elementary School, on Hamilton Street just off of Linden Street. I had a teacher there with whom I did not get along and who did not get along with me. As a result, I spent most of the time in the hall instead of in class. My first report card that year had something like thirteen Fs and eight Ds, which suggests that they had lots of subjects, like neatness, conduct, effort, penmanship, you name it. Apparently I was not good at any of them. The principal, Mr. Robert Rinker, and the teacher, Miss Grace Barthold, met with my parents, and they said, "Your son will probably never make it through junior high school. He has a learning disability and has serious problems, and there's not much we can do." As a matter of fact, the teacher said the only reason she passed me that year was that she was the only fifth grade teacher in that building, and she could not put up with me for another year. That was a second difficult experience early in my life.

But I made it despite their predictions. My parents saw that I needed help, so they hired Miss Gertrude Hafner, who had been the first woman principal of an elementary school and the first elementary school supervisor for the Bethlehem School District. To a fifth-grader, she seemed very old. She said, "Don't worry, Gordy will make it." She was always supportive, and I really needed that kind of support. With her help, I came back.

At the dairy, I learned to work in the garage and to service trucks. When I was fifteen, I was gassing the milk delivery trucks and driving them to where they were parked overnight, so they were ready for the next day. I know that Louie Durich, the man who was in charge of the garage, was very unhappy with me driving the trucks and filling them with gas; he was afraid I would be in an accident. Many of the trucks were stand-up Divco milk trucks, which were used by dairies to deliver milk when the driver had to make a lot of stops in a short distance. To make that easier, the trucks could be driven while standing up, and the clutch and the brake were in the same pedal. It is a miracle that I was never in an accident. Louie would say to my father, "You know, Mr. Mowrer, your son should not be driving these vehicles." My father would come to me and say, "Gordy, are you driving the trucks to the gas tank?"

Me: Yes.
Dad: You know, you shouldn't do that.
Me: Yes, I know that.
Dad: Well, then you really ought to stop.
Me: I'll be very careful.

And I would just ignore him and go on.

As I became sixteen, I worked in the trucks and garage department, and I delivered milk and ice cream all over the city by truck. I worked on the trucks going door to door, selling milk and butter and eggs and other dairy products. But my favorite job was working in The Cup.

For many years I worked in The Cup dipping ice cream. One Sunday after church, a man came in wearing a white suit. I was serving milkshakes to customers, and I accidentally tripped over somebody. I spilled a chocolate milkshake all over his white suit. Needless to say, I had to pay to get his suit cleaned.

At Christmas time, my brother and I made "snowballs" to sell. They were vanilla ice cream balls covered with coconut, with a small candle stuck in each ball. They were very popular as a dessert, and we made lots of them.

I learned a lot while I was growing up in the milk and ice cream business. I learned, for example, that when you own your own business, you work very hard, and you work every holiday. Every Christmas and every Easter, if somebody didn't get their milk or somebody else didn't get an ice cream order, they would call. My brother and I would answer the phone, and we would end up delivering those items. I learned that this was our livelihood, so I learned to take care of people, and I learned to care about people.

The Mowrer family has not been associated with The Cup since 1953, when the business was sold. The building was replaced with the Bethlehem Dairy Store, which still operates at 1430 Linden Street (and which is still called The Cup by many long-time Bethlehem residents). My wife and I still enjoy going there for ice cream, and often we take our family with us, including our grandchildren. In 1954, Mowrer Dairy merged with Suncrest Farms, to become the second-largest dairy in the Lehigh Valley. Eventually it was bought by Abbott's Dairy from Philadelphia, and was closed. The old dairy building has been converted into an office building.

One of my early friends was a fellow by the name of Russell K. Laros, Jr., whose father owned the Laros Silk Mill. As a boy, his nickname was Larry. I recently asked him why that was his name, rather than Russ, as he now calls himself. He said that his five older sisters wanted a name with alliteration for the new baby, and he thinks that there was also a movie star (or maybe a boyfriend) named Larry. Larry and I were born at St. Luke's Hospital at the same time and grew up together, served in each other's wedding parties, and have remained good friends to this day. We both currently serve on the board of the R. K. Laros Foundation, which his father established. Over the years, the Laros Foundation has given over $6.5 million to organizations in our community where there are special needs.

Russ "Larry" Laros *left* and I were childhood friends who did eyebrow-raising things together.

When Larry and I were young, we did all kinds of crazy things, the most notable of which was painting his German shepherd *green*. I think that we saw workers painting the shutters on his house, and we wanted to paint, too, so we used their green paint. I cannot remember why we selected the dog to paint. Many years later in 1987, I introduced Larry at the annual Bethlehem Area Chamber of Commerce dinner, at which he was the speaker, and we both recalled that incident. I know that when I first met them, his children were excited to meet the man who helped their father paint the dog green. We also tarred the side of a freshly-painted white house that was to be the new home for one of Larry's sisters and her husband following their wedding.

Larry's father had a Chrysler limousine, a big, black vehicle. Sometimes Larry would dress in a chauffeur's outfit, including the chauffeur's hat, and I would sit in the back seat. He would drive me downtown, and in front of the Bush & Bull department store (which became Orr's; the building is the Main Street Commons today), he would stop the vehicle, get out and open the door. I would get out and go in, and people would wonder who the heck we were. At the time we were sixteen or seventeen years old.

Despite the predictions of my elementary school principal, I managed to graduate from Liberty High School in 1953. Even in those days, I was a very determined person. I persevered, and when I really wanted to accomplish something, I gave it all the effort and energy that I had. I think I have continued to do that, both growing up and in my business and political careers.

My goal as a young man was to go to college, Dickinson College in particular. I wanted to come back with a Dickinson sweatshirt on and kind of rub it in the faces of my elementary teachers and say, "See, I made it and you said I wouldn't." (I wanted to, but I never really did it.) Because of my early experience with education, I have always been very helpful to people who have a questionable future because of their scholastic background. I know for a fact that many people have looked at me and said, "If he can do it, I can do it, too." I have tried very hard to inspire people who have struggled, giving them the support they need while making decisions.

I achieved my college goal. I was accepted at Dickinson, and I started there in the fall of 1953. My experience in college turned out to be a little different than most people might guess. I went to Dickinson feeling really good and loving the school very much. The first thing I did when I got on campus was to join the Kappa Sigma fraternity. I got to know people, and on weekends I didn't have to go to bed, because no one was watching me. Sometimes I would stay up all night; I had a wonderful time. The only thing I didn't do was study. I did not know how because I had never learned. I really was not ready for college.

At that time I was a pre-theological student, intending to go into the ministry, and I certainly thought God would help take care of me. When the first report card came out, I discovered I was second in my class – from the bottom. I had three Fs and two Ds, and I thought the world had come to an end. Even though I did not know how to study, I had never flunked a subject before. I got myself together and went to see the dean of the college.

Dean: Do you think you'll have a 2.0 average?
Me: Well, maybe not.
Dean: Do you know what you did wrong?
Me: Yes, I didn't study.
Dean: Do you think you can do better?
Me: Yes, I think I can.
Dean: We will let you come back to college next semester.

At that moment I knew that I would not have to call my parents to come and get me.

I returned to Dickinson and I did much better my second semester. They let me stay for a third semester, but I had learned that I really was not ready for college. The GI Bill was coming to an end. If I joined the Navy then, the government would help pay for my education when I returned to college. This is what I decided to do. I joined the Navy and went on board the USS *Valley Forge* for two years.

My Navy photo

In the Navy, I learned without any question that I wanted to come back to Dickinson and finish, to graduate from college and get a job where I could do something more than scrape the deck. While I was in the Navy, I worked in the Information and Education Office, helping people get their high school diplomas and GEDs, and often helping them start taking college courses. I took some myself, for which I got credit at Dickinson when I went back.

I reapplied to Dickinson after two years, and as part of the process I met with the academic committee. After the interview, one of the deans said to me, "I notice that when you took freshman English, which is grammar, you flunked it, and when you took it over, you only got a D." He continued, "In the past forty-five minutes while we've been interviewing you, I have noticed that you have not made one grammatical error. I don't know how you do it." As soon as he said it, I think I immediately started to make mistakes, because I started to think about what I was saying and what the words were, and whether I was right or wrong.

Dickinson accepted my return. I came back. This time, I served as a resident adviser for freshmen, which was considered a high honor. My goal now was to go from the dean's bad list, which I achieved my first semester, to the actual Dean's List, to change my first semester grade point average of .375 to a 3.75. I never quite made it, but I did reach a 3.5 average. The dean came to me at the end of my college career and he said, "Any time you would like a recommendation, I would be happy to give you one." And he did.

When I was a kid, we would go to watch Lehigh University wrestle in Grace Hall, which was quite an experience. I also had the opportunity, as a wrestler for Dickinson College, to come and wrestle in Grace Hall. I never was a champion wrestler like my father, but I did have the experience of

There was always a part of me interested in wrestling, because of my father.

wrestling at Lehigh, and what a marvelous experience it was. As a matter of fact, at Dickinson, the only trophy that I ever won was in 1958, when I was elected the Most

My parents, Clifton E. Mowrer, Sr. and Margaret Brown Mowrer, were very proud of me on my graduation from Dickinson. We posed outside Morgan Hall, where I was resident advisor.

The principals of the Hampson Mowrer Kreitz Insurance agency *left to right*: David Dyson, Gordon Mowrer, Tom Hartzell, C. E. "Tip" Mowrer, Jr., Bill Kreitz, George Mowrer.

Valuable Wrestler. I also got to captain the wrestling team from time to time.

I graduated from Dickinson in 1959. I was immediately hired by the A. B. Hampson Insurance Agency, then located at 35 E. Elizabeth Avenue in Bethlehem. The Hampson Agency was run by Arthur B. Hampson, and he hired me as his sole salesman to build a future for his agency. Over the course of the years, the agency has grown tremendously. In 1960 it became the Hampson Mowrer Agency. Eventually my brother, who was a great asset to me when I was mayor of the city, and my father also became part of the agency. My son, George, continues in the family business. I hired Bill Kreitz, who later became president of the agency and has done an extremely fine job; and I also hired David Dyson, who continued many of the traditions of our agency with people being involved in the community. Dave was president of the Bethlehem Chamber of Commerce, as was Art Hampson, my father, and me, all at different times.

Our employees were involved in the community; many of them got involved in Rotary and served as District Governors. I have been very involved with Rotary International for over 50 years. I have served as club president, I am a Past District Governor, and I am a Paul Harris Fellow.

Since 1994, the agency has been called Hampson Mowrer Kreitz Insurance. It is an agency that cares about the city and about people, and it is an agency that carries on the tradition which I hope that I was part of starting. I took a leave of absence from the agency during the years I was mayor, and I retired from the company in 1994.

When I first went to Dickinson, I was intending to be a minister. During my time there and in the Navy, I struggled with my beliefs. Eventually I changed my major to political science and looked toward a career in business. But even in business and later in politics, I ministered to people in the sense of attending to their needs, not necessarily in a religious sense. Politics turned out to be great training for the ministry.

I got my start in the ministry after I completed my first term as mayor. I served as a part-time pastor in a Methodist congregation in Johnsonburg, New Jersey in 1978 and 1979. I became a chaplain at St. Luke's Hospital in Bethlehem, serving overnight once, and sometimes twice, a month on a volunteer basis. I recently returned to that position; I now serve as a chaplain at St. Luke's for two mornings each week.

I returned to school, earning a Master of Arts in Pastoral Counseling degree from Moravian Theological Seminary in 1988 and a certificate in theological studies. I was ordained by the Moravian Church in 1992.

I served as a Moravian pastor for almost fifteen years. I was senior pastor of Advent Moravian Church, in Hanover Township just north of Bethlehem, from 1990-2002. During that time, we doubled our membership, doubled our physical plant, and paid off all of our debt. It was a wonderful experience. I also served as an interim pastor of the Midway Manor Moravian Church, on the border between Allentown and Bethlehem, in 2006 and 2007.

I met my wife, Mary, in 1960 on a blind date. Her name was Mary Thaeler. Her parents, Dr. A. David III and Margaret Heidenreich Thaeler, were well-known missionaries in Nicaragua for the Moravian Church. Her father was a medical doctor, and Mary was studying at St. Luke's Hospital to get her graduate degree in medical technology, so she could go back and open a laboratory for her father to do some medical research in the field of malaria. When I went out with Mary on our first date, I did not realize that she was about to announce her engagement to another person. I did not realize it until our third date, when she finally told me. Needless to say, I did what I consider to be the best sales job that I ever did in my life, selling her on my idea that the other fellow was not the one that she wanted; it was me that she wanted. I kept coming back. We were married in Nicaragua on December 29, 1960.

The Mowrer family at the Hotel Bethlehem, during a political fund-raiser for my first campaign: my brother Tip and his wife Barbara, my father and mother, myself and Mary

We have three beautiful children who have shared life and sometimes politics with us. George was born on September 6, 1963; Ruthie was born on April 7, 1966, and Meg came along on January 11, 1973, as I was running for mayor. (As a matter of fact, the night Meg was born, I was speaking at Moravian College.) They will have a chance to tell some stories later in this book. Our family also includes eight grandchildren, and over the years we have hosted many foster children and exchange students. Our house has always been filled with kids, most of them teenagers.

My early life had three major strikes against me: I was not supposed to survive my birth; my elementary principal and some teachers thought I would never get past junior high school; and I almost flunked out of college. But I managed to prove everyone wrong. I got my Bachelor's degree from Dickinson College, which is a fine school. I have a Master of Arts in Pastoral Counseling (MAPC) degree from Moravian Theological Seminary, as well as a Master of Education degree from Lehigh University. I ran a successful insurance business for over 30 years. And, of course, I became mayor of Bethlehem, the town where I grew up, serving from 1974 to 1977 and again in 1987.

At the reunion celebrating the 45th anniversary of my graduation from Dickinson College, Dr. William G. Durden, the president of Dickinson, said, "All our memories of what college was like are not real. They are our interpretation of what happened and our recollections as we remember them." This is what I intend to do in this book – to share my stories of the past as I remember them. Other people may not remember these events in the same way, but these are my interpretations and my memories.

Chapter

2

See Gordon Run!

The seeds of my running for mayor in Bethlehem were planted in 1969 in a psychology class which was taught by Dr. Theodore Millon at Lehigh University. He was the chairman of my graduate studies committee and a very influential person in my life.[1] In the middle of the class, Ted looked at me sitting about two-thirds of the way back and said, "Mowrer, you're never going to become a counselor." I said, "Well, if you know so much, what am I going to do?" He replied, "You're going to run for mayor of the city of Bethlehem." I said to him, "Whoever in their right mind would want to become mayor of the city of Bethlehem?" He answered, "You don't want that forever, but it would be a stepping-stone. You would run for mayor, and after you get that you would look for other opportunities, maybe become lieutenant governor as the Lehigh Valley begins to get recognition, and then you could move forward and take advantage of those new opportunities."

The more I thought about it as I traveled on my road around the Lehigh Valley, the more I thought that politics might very well be my calling. I had majored in political science at Dickinson College, so I had some knowledge of the field. I thought:

---

[1]Dr. Millon today heads the Institute for Advanced Studies in Personology & Psychopathology in Port Jervis, New York.

Dr. Ted Millon and I met regularly during my first campaign for mayor.

✓   I like people,

✓   I like doing things for people,

✓   I like being where the action is,

✓   I'm a pretty good administrator,

✓   I have lots of business experience,

✓   I can handle a busy schedule, since I am running a successful business while taking graduate work at school.

It looked interesting. The seed was planted.

When I ran for mayor the first time, in 1969, I was quite young. The first time I was elected, in 1973, I was 36 years old. In those days that was really considered young, especially for an elected official. When we ran against each other, Gordon Payrow treated me like an inferior, as though I didn't know what I was doing. In fact,

I remember that he used to look at me as if to say, "Just who do you think you are, challenging me? After all, I've been mayor for a couple of terms, and I've been around the block. I understand what's going on." The truth of the matter is that he was correct; it *was* pretty presumptuous of me to think that I could do better than an experienced elected official.

Gordon Payrow and I had over twenty debates, and at each debate where we met, the same person came and sat in the front row. While I was speaking, this person talked constantly, *out loud*, to throw me off and distract me. It was a great lesson for me, particularly later when I became a pastor and I had to focus on the sermon while some baby was crying, or some little kid was making all kinds of noise. I learned something from every experience.

In the beginning of my political career, I had to make some decisions. One of the decisions was how I was going to meet people and tell my story. I had to find some people who knew their way around the political world who would guide me and take me around and introduce me to folks in these settings. Dr. Charlie Zug and his wife, Dotty, were wonderfully helpful. Every night after campaigning, I would go to their house and we would debrief the day.

One way that the Democrats, particularly, politicked was to go to various clubs and bars and restaurants to meet people. Two of the people who helped me a great deal were John Schweder and Jack Collins. They knew people; knew all about campaigning; knew the bars, the restaurants, and the clubs, and were able to introduce me. For that, I was very grateful to them.

One of the experiences I had was with Jack Collins, who was the owner of the Old Brewery Tavern (OBT), on

Union Boulevard at Monocacy Street. Jack was very instrumental in teaching me to campaign around people. I vividly remember the first night he took me out. We went from club to club, bar to bar. He would have a beer, and I would have a mixed drink. To this day, I do not drink beer or coffee. I drank them when I was in the Navy, but when I got out, I said to myself, "Look, Gordon, you don't like beer and you don't like coffee, so quit drinking them." That night he had at least seventeen beers, and I had at least seventeen Seven and Sevens, a drink made of Seagram's 7 whiskey mixed with 7-Up. At the end of the evening, totally sober, I looked at him and said, "Jack, there's no way I can continue to do this or I will become an alcoholic." I decided that from then on, in my campaigning, I would drink plain ginger ale and most people would not know the difference.

Another way to meet people in communities was going to what were called neighborhood "coffee klatches." These events were very instrumental in helping me to know a lot of people. I would encourage people in neighborhoods to invite their neighbors and their friends over to their home and have a cup of coffee, and maybe a little cookie or something. Then I would have an opportunity to talk to these neighbors about who I was and why I was running, and then give them an opportunity to ask questions.

When people would meet me at one of these gatherings, often they would then go around and talk about me in the neighborhood, even though usually I had not known them beforehand. It was a marvelous way to get to know people, and it was very exciting to meet different people at different places.

Another way we used to campaign was going door-to-door. I often did this with other candidates, particularly

The buttons for my first campaign were six inches in diameter, so large that I thought no one would want them. Instead, they became collector's items. I still find them at garage sales every now and then.

when I was mayor and they were running for City Council. We would get together in the evening, walk down the streets and knock on the doors of registered voters who were on the party's priority list. They were called "SuperVoters," the people who had voted in the most recent elections.

One of the people that I campaigned with was a man by the name of Jerry Hargrove. He was a great big guy, black, a Golden Gloves champion, and a Baptist pastor. He was the nicest guy you would ever want to meet. When it got to be dusk, he would knock on the door, and sometimes if no one answered, he would look in the window of the front door to see if anybody was going to answer. I remember one time there was a little lady who was looking out the window just as he was looking in, and she kind of screamed, not knowing who was at her door. The little lady laughed when she realized what had happened, and there was nothing serious that resulted. Campaigning with him was kind of fun, and we appreciated his sense of humor.

Going door-to-door was a wonderful way to get to know people, and for that we were grateful. Sometimes when we would knock, we were invited to come into the house, and sometimes we would stand and talk with the people at the door, and occasionally they wanted nothing to do with us. For the most part, people really appreciated the fact that potential elected officials came and knocked on their door, cared about their neighborhood, and would listen to the problems and issues of the day that concerned them.

One of the ways to meet people was to go to the various clubs. When I first became involved in politics, there were many, many Democratic clubs. The Edgeboro-Pembroke Club was one of the largest. There were dinners, there were meetings, there were times to speak, there were opportunities to meet people; I would meet lots of people at the Edgeboro-Pembroke Club. Other clubs included the Jefferson, the Grover Cleveland, the Hungarian Catholic, the sokols, the Catholic sokols, the national sokols,[2] the Tammany, the Puerto Rican Club, the Heights Athletic Association. There was the Windish Hall, the Croatian Hall, and the Polish Hall. Wherever you went there was a Democratic club that sponsored dances and dinners and social activities for people to meet and talk. Many of our rallies were held in these clubs. We had many opportunities to go through and shake hands and introduce ourselves and tell people what we were running for and ask for their votes. I would meet a lot of people by going to these clubs.

---

[2]Sokols were organizations primarily for members of eastern European ethnic groups and churches. Originally they were founded to promote exercise and other noble causes. In South Bethlehem, they also became social clubs, especially for members of a specific church or ethnic group.

One of the interesting things about the Puerto Rican Club is that I knew a little bit of Spanish. When I would go there, I would give a little Spanish talk:

Me llamo Gordon, y quiero su voto para ser su proximo alcalde. (My name is Gordon and I want your vote to be your next mayor.)

or *Me llamo Gordon, y necesito su voto para ser su prixino alcalde.* (My name is Gordon and I need your vote to be your next mayor.) The Puerto Rican people loved it when I tried to speak their language. Even when I messed it up, the mere fact that I tried seemed to make a significant difference.

My favorite thing about the Polish Hall was their spaghetti dinners. Bucky Szulborski, a high school student at the time, used to eat half of my spaghetti and my son's and daughter's spaghetti as well. He could eat more spaghetti than anyone I knew.

Although Mary did not usually come with me when I went to these clubs, she did come to a number of the dinners and dances. On Saturday or a weekday night the Edgeboro-Pembroke Club often would have a dinner and then a dance. The Hungarian Catholic Club had a dance almost every Sunday night. We got to know many of the people in the club, and it was lovely. Today, almost none of the clubs are very active, and many no longer exist. But during the campaigns, we did a lot of socializing in the clubs.

One night, Mary and I went to a club on the South Side. After we had dinner, I said to Mary, "I'm going to go around to the tables and introduce myself as a candidate for mayor, to see if I can answer questions and let them know what they can do to support me." While I went around to some of the tables, Mary stayed back where we had dinner. Somebody who had obviously had too much to drink came up to her and said, "You know, lady, you have the most beautiful blue eyes I have ever seen." Well, her eyes are not blue, and she was not happy with the situation. She got out of there as fast as she could and ran over to the table where I was, and said, "Gordy, don't you ever leave me alone again!" She didn't always come with me to clubs after that.

Another thing I did to get to know people was to walk in the wards. Often I would walk with committeepersons, men and women elected from their district to represent their political party to their neighbors and friends in that district. We would go door-to-door, and they would introduce me personally to their friends. Nick Zanakos, an attorney in the 15th Ward on the North Side, took me around. We knocked on doors and he introduced me and recommended me to the people that he knew. George Dyonda, Sr., had been around for a long time and had walked the wards many times, and probably was as well known as anyone. He took me around and introduced me to people, and got his son, George Dyonda, Jr., involved in the campaign as well. It was fun walking with an older man who had been around the block, literally, many, many times.

Ernie DiSalvatore, from the 15th Ward, also took me door-to-door. He would also take me to softball games and the opening day of Little League. I would throw out the first ball, make a big production with a little speech, and meet the kids and their families. We would go everywhere and meet all kinds of people.

Ernie liked telling me and my wife what to do. For example, I used to call my wife "Mama Bear." Ernie thought it was a terrible nickname, that it was not as dignified as it should be. It was around the time that Lyndon Johnson called his wife Lady Bird, and my wife became Mama Bear. To this day she is often known as Mama Bear. Ernie worked hard for me and did a great job, and I value the experience of working with all the people who took me door-to-door and introduced me to new people.

Every time I could go through a factory of any kind, I took advantage of the opportunity. It was a chance to meet new people and to spread my name around as a candidate. I remember going through Just Born and having Jack Shaffer, the president, personally take me through and introduce me to people, encouraging them to support me in the election. It was a great experience. I learned about Just Born candy, I met some new people, and I had the opportunity to see one of the great industries in Bethlehem under the guidance of the head man himself. Jack was a wonderful person, and I have great memories of going through Just Born with him. Those were the days when the factory was not so automated, so it was a different experience than it is today.

I would also go through textile factories. We had many factories with sewing operators in Bethlehem in those days. I got to meet the ladies and learn what they made, to see all the products that were made in Bethlehem. One of my favorite stories of going through a factory was when I stopped by a lady who was at her sewing machine. I would usually give these workers a pack of matches with my picture on it, and I would say to them, "I hope you vote for me when you vote for mayor." This particular lady looked at the picture, and then she looked at me and she said, "Are you Gordon Mowrer?" I said that I was. She said to me, "You don't look anything like your picture." I asked her if I looked better or worse. Without any hesitation, she looked at me and said, "Oh, you look much worse in person!" I thought it was funny. But from time to time as I campaigned, I got lessons in humility that kept me on my toes.

I would go through factories where they made jackets, coats and all kinds of clothing. It was a wonderful experience to learn about Bethlehem and what is made there. In addition, these factories often had unions. It was important to get the support of the union, because the unions would actually take their members to vote, and recommend how they should vote as well. Factories were definitely on my agenda.

One of the early people that I got to know was a friend from way back in athletic programs, Charlie Brown. Charlie Brown went door-to-door on my behalf, wrote letters to his friends and people he knew, and was very supportive of me. Very honestly, I got to know Charlie as a result of that, and later on I hired him as a department head. In politics, there sometimes are appointments that go to people who work for you. I'm reminded of the story of what Mayor Richard J. Daley of Chicago is reputed to have said. Once when he was interviewed by the press, they asked, "Is it true that 50,000 people on the city's payroll are there because they did you political favors?" He responded with, "That's absolutely true, next question." Yes, there were numerous people that I hired because of politics, but that was not the main consideration. I wanted competent people first. Often the political people were also the qualified people. Competence had to be the primary reason.

For example, during the gasoline shortage in the early 1970s, citizens had to come to City Hall to get a chit to buy gas. Only certain gasoline stations could sell gas, and the lines were incredible; sometimes they would go around the block. Joe Antiga, who was the chairman of my campaign when I ran for mayor, was also the president of the Pennsylvania Association of Gasoline Dealers as well as the Democratic Party chair in Bethlehem. At one point, the only station in Bethlehem able to sell gas was the station he owned on West Broad Street. So when people would come to City Hall to get their ticket to buy gas, we were sending them to his station.

I knew Joe from before I was mayor, and I knew his qualifications, so when I needed someone for the job of organizing the gas chits, I thought of him. It was a volunteer position, not a paid one, but he benefitted from it. He did a good job, and obviously was qualified for the job, and it worked well. Politics does intersect with staffing from time to time, and occasionally people were appointed who also had political affiliations with the mayor.

In another case, I remember when one of the members of our staff was being interviewed for his first position with Bethlehem. He thought he wasn't going to get the job, because I had recommended someone else for an interview. My philosophy was that if you have worked for me, I will get you an interview, but you have to earn the job on your own. This particular fellow thought he would not get the job because I had not recommended him. But when it came time to choose who to hire, he was the one that the personnel director recommended, and he was the one who was hired. Over twenty years later, Jeff Andrews, now the City of Bethlehem's Water Supply Superintendent, is still telling that story. He was hired to work in the water department, and worked his way up. I have been given permission to share his story here.

Dad was always supportive of me. Here he congratulates me on winning the election for mayor. The tally board behind us was used to post election results in the days before computers. *Courtesy the Morning Call*

Another thing that I had to do was to raise money. There are a variety of ways a candidate can raise money in politics: have a party and invite people, send letters (or

Mary, Ruthie *left* and George congratulate me on my win. *Courtesy the Morning Call*

e-mails, in today's world) asking people to send contributions to campaign headquarters. One of the things that I decided to try was to get key people to raise $1,000 apiece (in those days, $1,000 was a lot of money to raise). I think I needed about $5,000 for my first campaign, which was a lot of money for a primary campaign at that time.

I went to one man who was well-known in the community, Bernie Cohen, who was a strong supporter of Gordon Payrow, the current mayor. He did not want to support me in the general election, but he was willing to support me in the primary because he did not like Phil Gahagan and Frank Muhr, my opponents in the primary election. Frank Muhr was well known for his years of service to the school district in Bethlehem, but he was also very conservative, and often voted against tax increases. Phil Gahagan was a union-endorsed candidate. He had a reputation for being very outspoken, and sometimes drinking a little bit more than he should. He was not particularly the kind of person some people wanted as our mayor. Bernie asked if I would be willing to accept money for the primary election, knowing that he would not support me in the general election. I needed money for both the primary and the general elections, but I figured I would worry about the money for the general election after I got through running in the primary. So I said yes.

Bernie Cohen said, "I will invite ten people over to my house. Would you be willing to come over and answer questions?" I said that I would. So one Saturday morning Bernie had ten people over to his house, invited me to come, and I went for a question-and-answer period. When we finished I left, and he asked them all if they would be willing to give $100 each to my campaign for the primary. They all agreed, and Bernie called me on the phone and said, "I have good news for you. They've all agreed to give $100 apiece, so we've raised the $1,000 that you wanted." Then he added, "But there's one condition that goes with it. We don't want you to put our names in your report to the courthouse, so that people do not know where you got your money. In other words, list that you received this money, but put it in somebody else's name rather than ours." They did not want Gordon Payrow to know that they were supporting me in the primary election.

I had a terrible time dealing with that. I was saying to myself that voters wanted me because I was an honest and ethical guy, and I did things right, and yet these men were asking me to falsify reports. I struggled with it over the weekend. Finally I called him back, and said, "Bernie, I want to thank you very much for your efforts. I feel really embarrassed to tell you that I decided that I can't do that. You're willing to give to my campaign because I'm honest and ethical, but then you're asking me to fill out a report that is not honest or ethical. I just can't do it." He hung up, but he called me back on the phone shortly thereafter, and said, "I've contacted all the men, told them what your predicament is, and what you're saying. We've all agreed that if you are going to fill out the report honestly, you may use our names, as long as you list it as people who have contributed to the primary and not the general." So I got through a major hurdle.

I cannot guarantee that every report that every treasurer has ever turned in with my name on it has listed every dollar according to where it actually came from, but the pattern was set. My campaign committee was going to be honest, we were going to be ethical, and when we had money to report, we were going to report it as coming from the person who gave it to us. And my campaign often limited the amount of money that we would accept from an individual person.

The first time I ran for public office I really didn't have any experience in government. I had to make up for that by emphasizing that I was youthful, I was experienced in running a business, I had talent, and I was willing to try new things. Bethlehem needed to move forward, and I was the man to make that happen. That was the mentality that Dr. Millon, who was meeting with me weekly, ingrained in me. He would suggest different thoughts and help me develop a foundation for my political platform. He helped give me some direction about what some of the issues were that were important to the people of Bethlehem, such as the influx of drugs into the Lehigh Valley, especially those problems that the present mayor was not facing or challenging.

When Dr. Millon, the other people who were advising me, and I put our advertising program together, we did so with the idea that we would use psychology to sell our campaign. We wanted people to identify with me, so we tried to use pictures of me in different situations. There was a picture of me in the Navy, so that people in the armed forces could identify with the fact that I had been in the armed forces, particularly if they were in the Navy. There was a picture of me at Emery Street gate at Bethlehem Steel, so that Bethlehem Steel people could identify with the fact that I was a member of CSL (I had worked on that crew, usually called the "labor gang," during college), and understood what it was like to clean out the flues and the furnaces and work for Bethlehem Steel. CSL was often described as the dirtiest, lowest-paying job in the plant, so it showed that I was willing to work hard. I also was a member of the union, and people could identify with me for that.

They could identify with me teaching at the community college. In my early career the community college needed instructors; since I had a master's degree in psychology from Lehigh, I could teach psychology at the community college. It was another way to tie in with the people who went to the community college. There was a picture of me working at The Cup, the dairy store which my father made famous back in 1930 as he put together the patent for The Cup's design. I had worked in The Cup for many years, and we wanted people to remember me. The purpose was to have people identify with me, so that they would be more likely to vote for me.

There was a picture of me with Miss Gertrude Hafner, my former tutor, who was the first woman principal in the city of Bethlehem. Gertrude Hafner and I were good friends. She tutored me when I was in fifth grade, when I was having some difficulty with school. We continued to be friends through my political years. I took her to vote on election day when she was ninety years old.

We also had pictures of me as a family man, including our two oldest children, Ruthie and George (our youngest daughter, Meg, was born during my second campaign). Mary, who was not politically motivated, really did amazingly well keeping the family going while I was out campaigning. She learned to take care of herself, and how to meet and talk with all kinds of people.

The campaign team used any manner possible to get out information about me. That even extended to handwriting analysis. A woman from Bethlehem was a certified graphoanalyst, and she wrote a column for the newspaper. In 1969, as I was running for mayor for the first

Every time I ran, Mary volunteered to stand outside on Election Day, no matter what the weather was.

time, some of her readers challenged local politicians to have their handwriting analyzed. I was one of the first to accept the challenge. Her letter to me, with her analysis, stated in part:

> ". . . You have ambition. You are broad-minded enough to see both sides of a problem . . . You are practical and unselfish, have the ability to influence people without domineering. In fact you do encourage others. You can speak when necessary and you can keep confidences.
>
> You have developed good basic leadership and apparently seek to establish plans which will require a consistent program of action to realize successful results. You can be depended upon to drive through to the completion of a project. Your dignity reflects your self-esteem.
>
> People could trust your direct manner – they would know where you stand, because you go directly to the point without subterfuge. You believe in getting right to the heart of a problem.
>
> Pride sets the standard for your integrity. It supports your desire to do what is right. You strive to live with honor. You like responsibilities and are always willing to learn."

I like to think that her analysis was correct, and that people felt that way when I was running for office. In my life, I have run three times for mayor of Bethlehem, and three times for member of City Council. My first campaign for mayor was in 1969, when I ran against Frank Muhr and Philip Gahagan in the Democratic primary. Frank Muhr was the president of City Council at the time, and Phil Gahagan was a lawyer in Bethlehem and involved with the union. I won that election, and I ran against Gordon Payrow in the general election, losing by 700 votes. Payrow was the incumbent, and had been the city treasurer before serving two terms as mayor. At that time, you were not limited to two terms.

In 1971 I ran for City Council and I won. Of the three candidates elected, I received the most votes. I served for two years, until I became mayor.

In 1973, as a member of City Council, I ran for mayor a second time. This time in the primary I was running against Charles Donches, who was president of City Council, and Joseph Mangan, a former member of City Council who was Bethlehem's director of parks and public property. I beat Charlie Donches by about 350 votes to win the Democratic nomination. Then I ran against Charles Chaffee, former superintendent of schools for the Bethlehem School District, and I won. I served as mayor of Bethlehem from 1974 through 1977.

In the primary in 1977, I ran against Paul Marcincin, the president of City Council, and Joseph Mangan again. Paul Marcincin won the primary. I did not run for mayor again, although I served for one year as mayor in 1987. I came back.

As a candidate, I always seemed to run against the president of City Council. Members of Council, including me, have always used that position as a stepping-stone to higher office. Even today, almost everybody on City Council wants to be mayor, and thinks they could do a better job than the current mayor. That meant that as mayor, I always dealt with a certain amount of jealousy or interference. So sometimes, in order to get my ideas passed, I used Joe Pongracz, the assistant solicitor for the city, a man who was respected by City Council, as one of my ambassadors to sell programs to members

When I was installed as mayor in 1974, I worked with these members of Bethlehem City Council.
front left to right: Paul Calvo, Paul Marcincin, Dolores Caskey
back left to right: Larry Kisslinger, Charlie Donches, Bill Collins, Frank Muhr

of City Council. There was always a little resistance to what I wanted to do as mayor, but in the end, the members generally voted with me. They made a lot of noise, but that was all it was.

After all, I reorganized the whole structure of city government in Bethlehem. I went in as a rookie, and they bought my restructuring. Not only that, but some of those programs and changes are still being used today.

I am proud to say that as I write this, I am still a part of Bethlehem's city government. I no longer want to be mayor – as they say, I've "been there, done that." But I

Chapter

3

Hits and Misses

In January, 1977, as I was beginning the final year of my first term as mayor, I wrote an article for the *Bethlehem Globe-Times* which briefly answered the question, "What is it really like to be mayor?" It was published as a commentary called "Hits And Misses." I think it gave a good summary of my time at City Hall up to that point, showing both what I felt were some of my achievements as well as some of the frustrations.

When I wrote it, I was still deciding whether I wanted to run for a second term or not. I eventually decided to run for re-election.

The article is reprinted here, with the permission of the *Express-Times*, as it appeared on January 17, 1977.

COMMENTARY

Hits And Misses

(Ed. Note — The Globe - Times has agreed to provide space on this page for occasional commentary from Gordon B. Mowrer, Mayor of Bethlehem. This is intended to give the mayor an opportunity to express his personal philosophies. As in the case of other columnists, these views may or may not be in agreement with Globe - Times editorial policies.)

. By GORDON B. MOWRER

A question asked of me on numerous occasions is: "What is it really like to be mayor." I have to honestly say the answer is a mixed bag in that there are times when being mayor is exciting, challenging, and a truly pleasurable and delightful experience. However, there are also times when being mayor is a very frustrating, depressing, and exasperating experience. Sometimes I actually ask myself if one of the requirements of being mayor is to be thickskinned and even masochistic.

Interestingly enough the major problems that I deal with in City Hall are often the easiest problems for me to handle personally. Sitting down with the police department and discussing crime is really one of the major problems in the city. Trying to come up with a new way of increasing our clearance ate and reducing the crime rate n Bethlehem is an exciting and hallenging kind of situation. When you are able to do something about a problem like this it s extremely rewarding and astisfying, i.e., the new team olicing and management by objectives program in our Police epartment, in my judgment, as made it one of the most outtanding police departments that you will find anywhere. I el really good about that because I was very much involved the decision - making process. Another very rewarding situation which has happened to me

since becoming Mayor is the number of dedicated and committed people we have working at City Hall. It is a joy and an extremely positive experience to work with so many of the employees in our City government who are honest, ethical, interested, committed, and devoted to their City and are willing to go the extra mile any day of the week to make it better.

Another area that is extremely positive, not only for me, but for my family, is the opportunity to meet so many different kinds of people and share in their ethnic customs and food, as well as their homes. As a person, in the last three years, I have grown tremendously. I have had many experiences that I will cherish as long as I live.

What are the most frustrating problems that I deal with as Mayor? Well, first I think developing a sense of balance between my personal idealism, i.e., working for what I believe is right and proper, and the reality of a political system that sometimes is not conducive to that kind of idealism.

For example, there are times when pressures are brought upon me to put a person in a job who is not qualified, almost with the threat that if you don't hire this person or that person you won't be re - elected.

That, of course, leaves you with the thought of what can I accomplish if I am not elected. This is a problem that I wrestle with constantly; but I made the decision early in my administration to put the City first and only hire individuals with the qualifications to do the job. If I don't get re - elected because of this, at least I will be able to live with myself.

A second problem that I find extemely difficult to handle is the two facedness of some people. Some individuals smile and are extremely pleasant to my face, but when I turn my back they cheap shot and become very uncomplimentary. This is extremely frustrating and often even depressing.

My basic philosophy has been to treat people as people, in that I try to be sensitive to their concerns as best I know how, and attempt to find ways of helping them. I do not base my judgments on their voter registration or what they can do for me. I find that people look at me not as Gordon Mowrer the person, but as Gordon Mowrer the Mayor; what can he do for me, can I maneuver him to do what I want. This is sometimes a very difficult situation to deal with.

Lastly, there are petty jealousies that often exist which I find sometimes almost impossible to deal with. One example of this is my relationship with City Council. I have two members of Council who are vindictive and, who will vote against me because it is my idea or program, and do not always give consideration to the city first.

I personally, as Mayor, do not know how to deal with people who are out to destroy rather than build. For me that is one of the most difficult problems I face as Mayor. Overall, however, I feel Bethlehem is extremely fortunate in that I believe most of our elected officials are, in fact, sincerely interested in doing what they believe is right for their city.

Also, another frustration that I will share with you is the effect of being mayor on my life personally. That is, what effect it has had on my personality and family life. I can assue you that my wife is not delighted that on her birthday I had to fly to Washington to try to get federal funds for a program for Bethlehem, and that on our anniversary I sit in budget hearings.

It is not pleasant for her to go shopping in the supermarket and have someone come up and blast her on a multi - colored Christmas tree or have someone call on the telephone with a complaint and take it out on her. This is not a pleasurable side of being Mayor. I enjoy now more than anything else the quiet moments that I have with my family away from City Hall.

I hope that in this brief commentary today I have given you a perspective of the job of Mayor, of the realities that I face day to - day. There are both positive and negative aspects of being a Mayor in any City and it is the balance between the two which becomes part of the decision making process of determining whether one wants to continue in political office. Whether I decide to run for a second term as Mayor, or not, the experiences that I have gained in the past three years have been most rewarding and have enriched my life greatly.

Commentary: Hits And Misses

(Ed. Note - The Globe-Times has agreed to provide space on this page for occasional commentary from Gordon B. Mowrer, Mayor of Bethlehem. This is intended to give the mayor an opportunity to express his personal philosophies. As in the case of other columnists, these views may or may not be in agreement with Globe-Times editorial policies.)

By GORDON B. MOWRER

A question asked of me on numerous occasions is: "What is it really like to be mayor." I have to honestly say the answer is a mixed bag in that there are times when being mayor is exciting, challenging, and a truly pleasurable and delightful experience. However, there are also times when being mayor is a very frustrating, depressing, and exasperating experience. Sometimes I actually ask myself if one of the requirements of being mayor is to be thickskinned and even masochistic.

Interestingly enough the major problems that I deal with in City Hall are often the easiest problems for me to handle personally. Sitting down with the police department and discussing crime is really one of the major problems in the city. Trying to come up with a new way of increasing our clearance rate and reducing the crime rate in Bethlehem is an exciting and challenging kind of situation. When you are able to do something about a problem like this it is extremely rewarding and satisfying, i.e., the new team policing and management by objectives program in our Police Department, in my judgment, has made it one of the most outstanding police departments that you will find anywhere. I feel really good about that because I was very much involved in the decision-making process.

Another rewarding situation which has happened to me since becoming Mayor is the number of dedicated and committed people we have working at City Hall. It is a joy and an extremely positive experience to work with so many of the employees in our City government who are honest, ethical, interested, committed, and devoted to their City and are willing to go the extra mile any day of the week to make it better.

Another area that is extremely positive, not only for me, but for my family, is the opportunity to meet so many different kinds of people and share in their ethnic customs and food, as well as their homes. As a person, in the last three years, I have grown tremendously. I have had many experiences that I will cherish as long as I live.

What are the most frustrating problems that I deal with as Mayor? Well, first I think developing a sense of balance between my personal idealism, i.e., working for what I believe is right and proper, and the reality of a political system that sometimes is not conducive to that kind of idealism.

For example, there are times when pressures are brought upon me to put a person in a job who is not qualified, almost with the threat that if you don't hire this person or that person you won't be re-elected.

That, of course, leaves you with the thought of what can I accomplish if I am not elected. This is a problem that I wrestle with constantly; but I made the decision early in my administration to put the city first and only hire individuals with the qualifications to do the job. If I don't get re-elected because of this, at least I will be able to live with myself.

A second problem that I find extremely difficult to handle is the two facedness of some people. Some individuals smile and are extremely pleasant to my face, but when I turn my back they cheap shot and become very uncomplimentary. This is extremely frustrating and often even depressing.

My basic philosophy has been to treat people as people, in that I try to be sensitive to their concerns as best I know how, and attempt to find ways of helping them. I do not base my judgments on their voter registration or what they can do for me. I find that people look at me not as Gordon Mowrer the person, but as Gordon Mowrer the Mayor; what can he do for me, can I maneuver him to do what I want. This is sometimes a very difficult situation to deal with.

Lastly, there are petty jealousies that often exist which I find sometimes almost impossible to deal with. One example of this is my relationship with City Council. I have two members of Council who are vindictive and who will vote against me because it is my idea or program, and do not always give consideration to the city first.

I personally, as Mayor, do not know how to deal with people who are out to destroy rather than build. For me that is one of the most difficult problems I face as Mayor. Overall, however, I feel Bethlehem is extremely fortunate in that I believe most of our elected officials are, in fact, sincerely interested in doing what they believe is right for their city.

Also, another frustration that I will share with you is the effect of being mayor on my life personally. That is, what effect it has had on my personality and family

This was taken in December, 1974, during the 1975 budget hearings. People were not very happy, as you can see from the expressions. We were not getting what we wanted from members of council. "Humbling of the Soul," I call it.
left: Erma Aubert behind Gordon Mowrer
middle row, front to back: Dan Fitzpatrick, Norman Allan, Joe Mangan, Bill Mitchell
back row, front to back: Bob Galle, Stanley Zweifel, Joe Trilli, Frank Gaugler, Sterling Miller, Jack Berk *(in very back)*

life. I can assure you that my wife is not delighted that on her birthday I had to fly to Washington to try to get federal funds for a program for Bethlehem, and that on our anniversary I sit in budget hearings.

It is not pleasant for her to go shopping in the supermarket and have someone come up and blast her on a multi-colored Christmas tree or have someone call on the telephone with a complaint and take it out on her. This is

Past and present members of City Council and mayors posed for this photograph in 1976.
front row, left to right: Walt Dealtry, Jack Lawrence, William Collins, Larry Kisslinger, Frank Gaugler
second row: Charles Donches, Paul Marcincin, Frank Muhr, Gordon Mowrer, Gordon Payrow, Earl Schaffer, Peter Rybak
back row: Paul Jani, Robert Gross, Clifton E. Mowrer, Dolores Caskey, Thomas Hudak, Ann Ardoline, Stanley Frantz, Anthony Sacarakis

not a pleasurable side of being Mayor. I enjoy now more than anything else the quiet moments that I have with my family away from City Hall.

I hope that in this brief commentary today I have given you a perspective of the job of Mayor, of the realities that I face day-to-day. There are both positive and negative aspects of being a Mayor in any City and it is the balance between the two which becomes part of the decision-

The Mayor's Office staff during my first term, shown in the mayor's office (note the red curtains) *left to right:* Donna Fitting, receptionist; Joan Schrei, secretary; Daniel Fitzpatrick, administrative assistant; Pat Kesling, service and information officer, and me in the front.

The mayor and some of the department heads, first term *left to right:* Pat Kesling, Frank Gaugler, Louis Szmodis, me, George Perhac, Joe Trilli, Bob Galle, Erma Aubert

making process of determining whether one wants to continue in political office. Whether I decide to run for a second term as Mayor, or not, the experiences that I have gained in the past three years have been most rewarding and have enriched my life greatly.

Chapter

4

Main Street Mayor

Looking back over my years as mayor, I believe the most significant contribution that my administration made was to redirect the development of the downtown area, to stop tearing down the old buildings and instead to restore and rebuild existing structures and facades.

In 1969, when I first ran to be mayor of Bethlehem, the downtown was in deplorable condition. It was disintegrating, stores were closed, and it was disgraceful. Gordon Payrow, the then-mayor, knew that this was the situation, and he knew that he had to do something. Along with Bethlehem Steel, the Bethlehem Chamber of Commerce and some other groups, he had hired a fairly prominent planning company called Clarke & Rapuano to come in, do a study of our downtown, and recommend a program of redevelopment. The same company had done a study back in the 1950s (along with Russell Van Nest Black) and produced what they called an *Interim Report* in 1956. In December of 1969, Clarke & Rapuano published their comprehensive *Center City Report.* Their concept was to come in and tear everything down, close streets, redesign the whole downtown, build two new department stores as anchors to each other, and put more stores in between. The idea was really to compete with Allentown and other shopping malls.

This "tear down and rebuild" plan was presented by a lot of cities back in the '60s, and this is what Gordon Payrow used against me in the election in 1969. Even though the final report was not published until shortly after the election, he promoted his new plan when he was campaigning. People were just happy to see that something was being done. I was thinking about what to do with the downtown, but during the campaign I had no official plan to push. I lost the election by only 700 votes, which indicated that it would not have taken much to turn the election around.

However, I lost, and so I did what a lot of people told me to do: run for City Council, get some experience, and then run for mayor again. I was elected to the Bethlehem City Council in 1972, and I served for two years until 1974, when I began my first term as mayor. As a member of council, I learned first-hand how badly Bethlehem was on its way downhill in its development. People were saying that we needed to do something, anything, and so the Payrow administration promoted this Clarke & Rapuano plan. I even supported it when I was on City Council by voting to close Broad Street. (Yes, I will admit that I was a part of the closing of Broad Street, which was very controversial from day one.) But I realized in the process and in my travels that this was not the way to go for Bethlehem.

The Chamber of Commerce used to offer trips to various cities. Initially they went with just the men, but later they had trips when they went with men and women. I traveled with them during my first two years on City Council to different cities: to Atlanta, where we saw the early downtown storefronts which had been covered over by raised streets, and they restored the area very creatively with an underground mall called the Underground; to Alexandria, Virginia, where we saw a lot of the historic buildings which had been redone; to Puerto Rico; to Washington, D.C.; to Omaha, Nebraska, where we saw Air Force One; and to many U.S. Conference of Mayors cities, where I saw what different people did.   I would go to these places where I could see these creative programs put together. People developed ideas for making something that didn't look so good into something that really *was* good, and it made a big difference.

When I came home to Bethlehem after these trips and I walked around the streets, it did not take very long for me to come up with a solution. I said to myself, "There's only one thing Bethlehem has to sell, and that is history! The uniqueness of Bethlehem is our history; that's what we have to sell, and if we try to sell anything else we are going to fail. Bethlehem is not a shopping center, it is not a modern brand-new community, we are an old city that has charm and delight, and we need to sell that." We already had charming old buildings, and we needed to focus on them, to revitalize and reconstruct our downtown.

Another advantage was that we had a very good stock of housing in the downtown. Some of the finest housing in Bethlehem is all within the downtown area, which is very unusual for most cities in Pennsylvania, because the housing downtown is usually older and deficient. Bethlehem's housing downtown is outstanding. You can go within a short distance of the downtown and you can find some of the nicest houses in Bethlehem, in very charming areas to walk around.

An important part of my vision was hiring the right people to make it happen. Soon after I was elected mayor in 1974, I looked for a new city planner. I wanted somebody who had some experience with history and maybe with the redeveloping of history or redoing older cities. That's when

These artists' renderings showed how Main Street would look after the renovations were complete.

I came across Sam Guttman, and I hired him as the planner. We went around to more cities and studied what they had, and Sam showed me the importance of redoing existing buildings, which was very intriguing to me. It reinforced my feeling that the only thing that Bethlehem had to sell was its history. The buildings that we already had here should not be ripped down to build a new department store or a new shopping mall.

Sam Guttman was able to hire an organization called National Heritage Corporation from West Chester, Pennsylvania. John D. Milner, the president of the company, and his team came in and put together a master plan that redesigned Main Street, including the restoration of the Sun Inn and other parts of downtown Bethlehem. They realized that, although the south part of Main Street encompassed over 200 years of history, and the Moravian history was very significant to the development of the downtown area, much of the architecture of Main Street between Church and Broad Streets had evolved from those eighteenth century beginnings. The buildings mostly represented the Victorian period, rather than Colonial architecture.

National Heritage developed a comprehensive concept for what the redeveloped Main Street should look like. They specified how the building facades should be treated to maintain their unique qualities but at the same time promote a uniform, coordinated look which built on the town's history. They changed the look of the streets, intersections and sidewalks using cobblestones and bricks to make them more pedestrian-friendly, to encourage people to stroll through the downtown and look at the shops. They designed parking spaces and recommended the types of trees and plantings to use. They chose street lights, benches, litter receptacles and other street furniture to support the concept. They recommended that period signage, following certain guidelines, replace the hodgepodge of uncoordinated signs, which was detracting from the overall look of the downtown. They treated the whole environment, both the public portion and the private buildings, to create the overall image of a restored Main Street. The flagstones and the bricks and the intersections that they proposed were just as charming as they could be. Their report designed what I think turned out to be my legacy, the restoration of Main Street.

As we were working on these plans for redeveloping the downtown area, Bethlehem Steel hired a group called ULI – the Urban Land Institute, with headquarters in Washington, D.C., to do a second study of the downtown. The city government was making a major shift in philosophies, and Bethlehem Steel wanted another expert opinion. In the spring of 1976, a panel from ULI visited Bethlehem, and they published *Recommendations for the Revitalization of the Downtown Business District for the City of Bethlehem, Pennsylvania.* One of their conclusions was that "The commercial and office redevelopment called for in existing renewal plans [the 1969 Clarke & Rapuano report] has very little chance of realization . . ."[1] They were very enthusiastic about the Main Street plan that we were developing:

> "The Main Street renovation is a brilliant concept which can act as a catalyst to other downtown revitalization activity and as a unifying force . . . Those who originally conceived this idea, and especially the people in city government who selected so sensitive

---

[1] *Recommendations for the Revitalization of the Downtown Business District for the City of Bethlehem, Pennsylvania,* March 28 - April 2, 1976. A Panel Service Report by ULI – the Urban Land Institute, p. 11.

and competent a consultant firm as the National Heritage Corporation to give form and substance to the idea, are to be commended."[2]

A part of the Clarke & Rapuano plan which still retained some interest at the time was building a hotel and convention center complex in the downtown area north of Broad Street. The plans included a performing arts center and auditorium. While the ULI report did not find that the convention center would be successful, they recommended building the performing arts center south of Broad Street, at the corner of Guetter and Walnut Streets, close to the planned Walnut Street parking garage.

The initial money for this arts center came from the state because of Governor Shapp and his recognition of what we in Bethlehem had done to help get him re-elected. After the election was over, Governor Shapp said, "I'm here to help you in any way like you helped me."

So I went to Harrisburg to meet with the governor. I went with Dan Fitzpatrick, my administrative assistant, and Dan Church, who was a reporter for the *Globe-Times*. When I got there the governor would not allow the other two to join me, so I met with him privately. At the time the big issue was the SEPTA strike, and the governor was terribly involved with trying to resolve the strike in Philadelphia and getting people back to work. I thought to myself before I met with him, there's no way he's going to be able to focus on $1.5 million for the City of Bethlehem for a performing arts center. Amazingly, he sat down with me and we talked.

---

[2]ULI *Recommendations*, p. 20.

When Governor Shapp visited Bethlehem, we showed him around the area of the Main Street project, including the front of Central Moravian Church.

Governor Shapp agreed that he wanted to support me, and that he would tell the budget secretary to find the money in the budget for me. The budget secretary later confirmed this. The governor eventually announced that this money was going to come to Bethlehem, probably for a performing arts center off of Broad Street close to Main Street.

I think one of the reasons that Governor Shapp was interested in this performing arts center and the arts is because he himself played the violin, and was quite an accomplished violinist. There were other members of his family who were involved in the arts. So when the opportunity to support the arts came, the governor was right in our corner. I interviewed the governor for my WGPA radio program in October, 1976, and he commented,

> "I think civilizations are known for their culture. Unfortunately, for too long in Pennsylvania, there was an attitude that Pennsylvania is known for its smokestacks. And yet it's the culture that we develop in the arts – recreation plays a big part in that as well. But music, drama, dance, art itself is a very important part of life, and it should be even more important for more people. And so when we can put a theater right in the downtown of a city . . . it helps mold the whole character of downtown Bethlehem as part of the rebuilding program, it serves a double function. So I hope that you're using that theater, and will use it when it's finished . . . for a lot of functions that will be beneficial to the people here."

Needless to say, that performing arts center did not make it. Tom Maloney was the legislator who initially helped save the state money for Bethlehem when Senator Jeanette Reibman wanted it to go to another area of her constituency. The year after I left office, in 1978, Michael Schweder, who was then our representative, came forward and facilitated transferring the funds from the performing arts center to the restoration of the Sun Inn and also the Luckenbach Mill.   So the City of Bethlehem still benefitted from over $1.6 million from the state, and the Sun Inn was saved for downtown Bethlehem.

Even though the arts center was never constructed, I am happy to see that the open courtyard which occupies the site today is often used for small outdoor concerts, achieving the original purpose without walls. And in the more-than-thirty years since Governor Shapp spoke of culture in downtown Bethlehem, other facilities have been built to fulfill his dream of developing culture. The Touchstone Theatre on the South Side, the Payne Gallery and Foy Concert Hall on Moravian College's Priscilla Payne Hurd Campus at the south end of Main Street, Lehigh University's Zoellner Arts Center, ArtsQuest's Banana Factory on the South Side and the performing arts center at SteelStacks, all serve to, as he said, "mold the character" of Bethlehem and the area.

The idea of restoring the existing buildings to bring back the Victorian feeling was very intriguing to many people. Initially when we got the proposal for Victorian lights, I thought nobody on City Council would like them, because they were so different from what we had. However, much to my amazement, City Council loved them. They had the charm that we had been looking for, and it made a difference in our redevelopment in the downtown area. The people *loved* the idea. They loved the process. Suddenly, Bethlehem was unique, Bethlehem was special, Bethlehem was really the jewel of the Lehigh Valley. Bethlehem had it all, and everybody wanted this historic feeling.

I was excited about it, and so were some of the merchants. George Ramonat, who owned Tiger Hall, a men's clothing store, was one of the first to step forward and say, "We'll step up and redo our building so that it matches the style of the downtown." George Zajacek was another one; he was an architect, and he was very enthusiastic and supportive. Barry Pell and James Whildin, architects with Spillman Farmer Architects, redid their building. The Moravian Book Shop followed suit, and the Sun Inn had its stone walls restored.

We had some merchants who were not terribly cooperative. Fordham Bixler liked the big awning on his store, the old Bush & Bull building at the corner of Broad and Main Streets (now Main Street Commons). It was said to be one of the longest awnings in the world. But the next owners of the building restored its facade. Gradually, the stores and some new owners who took over some stores all seemed to want to be a part of it. It was exciting to see a new Bethlehem emerge, and all of a sudden we had a new city.

More people fixed up their buildings. The Central Moravian Church was acquiring property next to the Book Shop, and they fixed up more. Some people fixed buildings and brought new businesses there, like the man who followed me as mayor in 1988, Ken Smith, and his wife Barbara, who bought and restored a children's store in downtown Bethlehem. Moravian College and the Laros Foundation took the white paint off of the Single Brethren's House, which was the anchor at South Main Street. And the college put a lot of money into their southern campus to make it a more substantial part of their academic campus.

Those efforts are continuing even today. When AlphaGraphics, a business located in the former Weinland's Hardware building at the corner of Broad and Main Streets, burned down in 2005, Ashley Development Corporation bought the building and fixed it up pretty much the way it

The uniqueness of our city was buildings like the Sun Inn, shown here in 1976 at its reopening before the restoration. Hughetta Bender *in doorway, left,* led the effort, and I encouraged her and offered my help. *Courtesy Sun Inn Preservation Association*

Hughetta Bender welcomed Gov. Milton Shapp *center, back to camera* and me to the Sun Inn in the early stages of its restoration. *Courtesy Sun Inn Preservation Association*

was originally. At least it gave you the illusion of being one of the buildings of the older Victorian time.

While some buildings were being refurbished, other buildings were being rehabilitated or preserved. Restoring the Sun Inn had been recommended by the Clarke & Rapuano report, and all the subsequent studies agreed. The 1758 Sun Inn, at the northern end of Main Street, was built by the Moravians just outside of Bethlehem, so that visitors could stay there and be suitably entertained without disturbing life in the closed community. Many well-known Colonial-era travelers dined or spent the night there, including George and Martha Washington, the Marquis de Lafayette, John Adams, and members of the Continental Congress, who met there in 1777.

Hughetta Bender took on the challenge of restoring this building, and formed the Sun Inn Preservation Association, along with other people like Mike Schweder and Tom Maloney. In 1974 the city was able to give them $25,000 from a community development grant to help them purchase the building. There was talk of making the building into an upscale restaurant, although some studies questioned whether it was suitable for that use. The history of the building has proved that both sides were right: it has been used as an upscale restaurant, but often with great difficulty in sustaining it or making a profit. Nevertheless, it is an important building to have downtown.

The National Heritage plan also included the possibility of reconstructing two original Moravian buildings, the pottery and the forge, at the top of the hill across the street from Central Moravian Church. Although nothing was done about those buildings for many years, that suggestion was

The idea behind the skating rink in front of First Valley Bank was to have a little Rockefeller Center, complete with a Christmas tree in season. It was a great concept. We did have some trouble with the ice skating rink, but when it worked it was really kind of cool.

Enjoying the new Broad Street plaza are *left to right* me, Bernice Leder, Mort Baum and Larry Leder.

finally carried out in 2004, when the Historic Bethlehem Partnership completed a working replica of the Moravian blacksmith shop on its original site.

People came to Bethlehem and said, "This is charming, this is delightful." They walked the streets, and people felt at home. It had an atmosphere of not being a busy enterprise, like a big department store. The stores started to be rented, and people started to come to downtown Bethlehem. Today the street still displays a unique character. I believe that the restoration of the existing buildings in downtown Bethlehem has made all the difference.

James J. McCarthy, Jr., who was a senior planner for the City of Bethlehem during this time, has pointed out that in choosing this plan for the city, Bethlehem was in the forefront of a major national trend. In the late 1960s and early '70s, there was a shift away from a government program called "Urban Renewal," which demolished many decaying but historic sections of urban areas across the country, to a program focusing on the redevelopment of existing communities and properties. In a recent conversation with me, he said that "It was fantasy to believe that [Bethlehem] had the economic resources, going forward, to carry out anything like [the plans recommended in the report by] Clarke & Rapuano, whether we thought it was good or bad. The main thing that happened in [the Mowrer] administration was the whole direction changed, the way that the downtown was viewed."

Let me go back to the Clarke & Rapuano plan, and what they were projecting. There were some good ideas in it. One of them, frankly, was the ice skating rink in front of one of the anchor buildings at the intersection of Broad and New Streets, which was to be modeled after Rockefeller Center in New York. The plaza was intended to be a place where you could come and watch your kids ice skate, with the little Plaza Mall where people could talk, and at Christmas time we had a Christmas tree, just like Rockefeller Center. That area really looked nice in the center of town; there was a place for people to sit and be comfortable. The Bethlehem Plaza Mall, which became The Marketplace, in downtown Bethlehem never really made it as a shopping center, although later it made it as an office space. It did reach its ultimate goal, which was to bring people downtown. But probably the most controversial thing that ever happened in our downtown was the closing of Broad Street, on which the whole Clarke & Rapuano plan was based. At this point it is too late to debate it because it was closed, it was later reopened, and it has been successful since it has been reopened.

The Christmas tree next to the skating rink, on the plaza, was called the Mayor's Tree. In 1976, we put multi-colored lights on it for the first time, and added silver balls, and it was really a spectacular tree. I took a tremendous amount of abuse because of this tree. People wrote in the newspaper, "Is Gordon Mowrer Mickey Mouse? Is Gordon Mowrer Donald Duck?" This was all because when I went down to Disney World, I brought this idea back with me. The other trees on the North Side of Bethlehem all had white lights, and this one didn't fit the mold. The trees on the South Side were the ones with multi-colored lights.

When we were lighting the tree for the first time that year, the question came up whether we would be allowed to read a poem that my wife wrote in response to some of the controversy over white versus multi-colored lights. For the tree lighting on November 28, 1976, she wrote:

We gather this evening in Bethlehem,
To witness a glorious sight.
Though our thoughts are many, our motive is one
To turn on the Christmas lights.

And as we sing out our carols of joy,
May our prayers reach up to the heights
That the peace and the spirit of that first Christmas
   dawn
May be ours on this special night.

So now as we turn to put on the power,
And again see the spectacle bright
May the warmth of the colors fill our hearts with their
   glow.
Who cares if they're red, green or white.[3]

Mary T. Mowrer

They used to tell the story of the Christmas light controversy on the Chamber of Commerce's holiday bus tours of Bethlehem. When they got to the tree they told how this was the Mayor's Tree, and it had multi-colored lights instead of white, and ever since that tree, he was never able to get elected again. The story is attributed to Laurie Gostley-Hackett, who admitted to me that she started it. It made a great story, but the tree probably did not affect the next election.

There's no longer a Mayor's Christmas Tree there. Or a skating rink.

Christmas in Bethlehem has always been special with trees. In its heyday back in the 1940s, people used to line

---

[3]Reprinted with permission of the author

With Broad Street closed, there was plenty of room for benches so that people could sit and talk. During the Christmas season, the trees were decorated with white lights. *Courtesy the Morning Call*

up to see Bethlehem at Christmas time. Every lane of the Hill-to-Hill Bridge was solid with cars, with the exception of one lane which was left open for emergency vehicles. It was kind of an exciting time in Bethlehem back then, and it still is an exciting time in Bethlehem.

We had many Christmases in our downtown area, with Bucky Szulborski coming and playing Santa Claus in the mall. I used to take my kids in to town for the occasion, and lots of other people took their kids in, and we used to have a really good time together. It was a family celebration.

One new idea that was brought to us involved Hans Wuerth of Moravian College, who was a big bicycle enthusiast. In 1974, I had recently come back from Europe, where I saw that they had bicycle paths. During the early 1970s there was a national gasoline shortage, including a

Here I am arriving at the office on Church Street. We were strong supporters of bicycling and environmental concerns back in the '70s, and we put in bicycle paths. They were extremely controversial, and some people wanted to crucify me for putting in the bicycle paths. We put them in, and interestingly enough, the concept has returned.

time when if you wanted gas you had to come to City Hall to get a ticket to purchase it. We decided that bicycle paths would be good for Bethlehem. We laid out a four-mile loop in the downtown area, the first of its kind in Pennsylvania. More miles were added the next year.

Bicycle paths turned out to be one of the most controversial things that I did, and I got a lot of criticism for being willing to bring something so erratic to the city of Bethlehem. Some people loved them, and others hated them. We actually gave cyclists a lane solely for bicycles. In more recent years, Bethlehem has painted signs indicating that bicycles should share the lane with cars. Maybe that is a more conservative method. Probably ours were so controversial because some of our bicycle paths did take up some parking spaces. But the idea was to make riding a bicycle easier, to save energy. I myself used to ride my bicycle from our home on Bridle Path Road to work at least once a week. On hot days, though, it was not so good: I would ride into work and by the time I got to the office I needed to take a shower so that I didn't smell bad for the rest of the day.

In 1974, the federal government created the Community Development Block Grant (CDBG) program, which made funds available to redevelop existing neighborhoods and properties. This helped to move the focus away from demolishing buildings under Urban Renewal. The CDBG funding made a significant difference in the downtown revitalization. The Main Street project was basically funded with two grants, some funds from the Economic Development Administration and the remainder from the community development funds. The city hired a couple of young guys to work with Mullin & Lonergan Associates, Inc., our consultants on grants and funding, to let us know when we could and could not spend money. Jim McCarthy was one of those, and Frank Gaugler joined the city in that category. Dolores Caskey and Paul Calvo were strong supporters on City Council. We had key people and they worked to make it all happen. Today we look back, and people say, "Bethlehem was way ahead of everybody else."

The unfortunate part about our downtown project is that I did not get to be mayor when it was completed. I lost the primary election in May, 1977, but I did help to break ground for the Main Street project shortly before I left office

We broke ground for the Main Street project in December, 1977, just before I left office. Operating the jack-hammers are Dolores Caskey, myself and Franklin Gaugler. In the background are George Ramonat, George Hall, and Mort Baum.

at the end of 1977. It was mostly symbolic, because actual construction began a few months later. Fortunately, the new mayor, Paul Marcincin, agreed with my ideas about downtown redevelopment. The project was actually finished in Paul Marcincin's first year in office. However, that really doesn't matter because I was doing what I thought was right, and I was committed to it. My administration brought the plans in, we got it started, we got it funded, and we are very proud of what has happened since.

Each of the mayors after me, whether it was Paul Marcincin or Ken Smith or Don Cunningham or John Callahan, has continued the process of completing one block after another. Each of them did their part. And one of the unique qualities of Bethlehem is we have had consistently good mayors who have cared about the city and worked hard to make it all possible. I did my piece, and I say thank you for the privilege of having served.

When I step back and look at the development of the downtown area of Bethlehem, and in particular the emphasis on the historicity and its impact, I see three significant factors which are continuing to make a difference.

The first one is the Historic Bethlehem Partnership (HBP), formerly Historic Bethlehem, Inc., which has consistently worked to restore and preserve some of the old buildings, make them historically authentic and legitimate, and maintain them well.

Second is the impact that Moravian College and Theological Seminary has had on the downtown buildings. Whether you refer to the past work on the Brethren's House or to the latest dormitory that has just recently been completed on the south campus, it has had an incredible impact.

The third factor has to do with the development of the Sun Inn. Unfortunately, the Sun Inn has been unable to work together with HBP to benefit everybody. There is no question in my mind that the people who have been involved with the Sun Inn, starting with Hughetta Bender, going to Bucky Szulborski and Anne McGeady and others, have worked hard to establish what they felt was right. It would be my hope for the future that the historic organizations would be able to work together.

Even though I did not get to see the Main Street project completed in my term, I still won an award for the plan. In 1976 the Pennsylvania Planning Association (PPA) named me the Elected Official of the Year in the area of planning.

Three of the main architects of the downtown redevelopment *left to right,* Jim McCarthy, Frank Gaugler, and Sam Guttman, look over the plans of Main Street.

In presenting the Citation of Merit, the PPA chairman explained the plan that resulted in the recognition of my

"... leadership efforts in integrating planning and historic preservation efforts in directing the future development of the City of Bethlehem ... As in many major cities, the planning and preservation efforts have had rather different orientations. Planning in Bethlehem was oriented originally towards a longer-range strategy of central city redevelopment with a major emphasis on clearing land for new development. Preservation, however, was concerned only with maintaining the historic character of this eighteenth century Moravian settlement.

But during recent years while the mayor was in office, a critical need surfaced to develop a CBD [Central Business District] plan which would merge the planning and historic preservation efforts, to link a number of groups, both public and private, into various aspects of historic preservation with the broader goal of planning for an improved Central Business District. These efforts have been noted as particularly significant in this Bicentennial Year . . . [through] a creative linking of the present with that past. Mayor Mowrer's leadership has helped make that link work in a rather creative manner, and for that we would like to cite his efforts."[4]

When I look at my own record at City Hall – I was only really there five years in all – I can honestly say that the one thing that I would want to be remembered for would be the downtown revitalization. It was the imagination that I had, and hiring the right people to make it happen, that made us able to look back on what Bethlehem had to sell and sell it. As I said in my acceptance speech for the Planning Association award, "When elected officials and planners and planning offices work together, it's only under these circumstances that we recognize our true roles, that we really can accomplish great things for our cities."[5]

[4]Pennsylvania Planning Association award ceremony transcript, 1976.

[5]Pennsylvania Planning Association award ceremony transcript, 1976.

Chapter

5

Bethlehem's Best in Blue: The Police

The crime rate in Bethlehem when I became mayor was the highest it had ever been. I remember thinking to myself that if I were a regular citizen, the first thing I would do would be to go to the mayor and say, "What are you going to do about crime in the city of Bethlehem?" The city had been hit with a great deal of crime and drugs were starting to creep in. I said to myself, "This has to be a priority, because we must make this city a safer place to live."

I brought fresh air and fresh ideas and youth to City Hall. I hired young people, and I reorganized key elements of Bethlehem's city government. When I was elected in 1974, Bethlehem had a Public Safety Department, under Irv Good, which oversaw police and fire and ambulance and the city planners and more. I noticed that sometimes there were some conflicts between fire and police, so we divided them into two separate departments. We also created a Community Development Department, focusing on the potential for obtaining grant money specifically for programs in community development. My team changed the whole ball game.

My administration created a separate Police Department so we could focus more directly on every issue that had to do with crime and police work. I appointed H. Robert Galle as Commissioner of Police, and Stanley Zweifel as Deputy Commissioner of Police, and said to them, "I want change. Go and change the department," and they did.

There were two areas that were emphasized under my leadership. First we established the "management by objectives" (MBO) program, bringing in outside consultants to advise the police on this management technique. In other words, when we set the goals and objectives that we wanted the department to accomplish, we set specific goals and objectives that were quantifiable, that could be measured. For example, one goal might be "to reduce crime by 10% per year over the next three years," rather than just "we will reduce crime." We did not have to guess whether we had reached our goals with this program. There was a real spirit within our police department to work together and to make this program work. All the police officers studied "management by objectives" with a Penn State University professor, Dr. Samuel DeWald, through a management development contract with Penn State's Continuing Education program.

The second thing that was emphasized was the idea of team policing, a new approach that divided the police force into three teams. Begun in May, 1976, Bethlehem was the first city in Pennsylvania to use this concept. We had Adam, Baker and Charlie teams. Each team was responsible for a different section of the city. They would get to know the people in that neighborhood, and the people would get to know them because it would be the same officers coming back each time. The residents and the police would be able to work with each other. Over time, it made a difference

H. Robert Galle, the police commissioner, and I explain team policing.

in the crime rate, which was reduced dramatically, and in how the police department was viewed. As a result of the new approach, the police communicated more openly and directly with the public, and there was a more positive police presence in the community. Change was occurring in the police department.

One of the things that I enjoyed doing as mayor was riding in the police cars with the officers, hearing what was going on in the streets, watching some of the things that they had to put up with, and seeing for myself what was happening. It seemed to me that there was an incredible number of domestic calls. Whenever I was in a police vehicle, we always had several domestic calls where husband and wife were having problems, or parent and child were having problems, and they needed a police officer to break it up. I also saw a large number of calls having to do with neighbors; one neighbor was not getting along with another neighbor, and someone called the police to intervene. These calls dealing with domestic and neighborhood problems were very serious, because someone could be so mad they might pull out a gun and shoot somebody. At other times someone was hurt or in a fight or something else would go wrong. The police really had to be on guard, prepared for whatever might be happening.

Other calls would be as the first responder for an ambulance call. The police would usually arrive first on the scene, perhaps when someone was having a heart attack, or had committed some act of violence and someone was injured. Whatever was going on, the police were the first call. Although it was exciting, it was also very dangerous. I enjoyed going on those calls and seeing what the officers did.

My favorite story about my involvement with the police when I was mayor was the time that I went on a drug raid. The department knew that drugs, like "speed" and LSD, were available in Bethlehem. The police were fighting drugs as much as they could. They had planned a drug raid in the Marvine-Pembroke area, and I said, "I'd like to come along." The officers gave permission for me to join them.

We met about four o'clock in the morning. It was pitch black as we got ready to go out, because we tried to catch the dealers while they were still in bed. Everyone had to put on a bulletproof vest. Police always assume that drug dealers have guns, and that they are not afraid to shoot when a police officer comes to arrest them. Someone handed me a bulletproof vest. But the difference between my vest and everyone else's vest was that there was a hole in mine. On a previous occasion, someone had shot through this vest, which turned out not to be bulletproof. I am not sure exactly what happened because they did not tell me the rest of the story. But I wondered how I "happened" to get the one with the hole in it. I thought that maybe someone was giving me a message. Fortunately, whether the "bulletproof" vest really worked or not was not tested during this raid.[1]

We all drove over there as quietly as we could. As we were getting out of our vehicles, word of our plans spread, and suddenly there were people crawling out the windows of the second floor. There was a young man up there, probably in junior high school, and he looked down and saw me and yelled, "Hey, Gordy!" I looked up, and here was a boy to whom my son had been a Big Brother. He had been in my house; that was the connection. I do not think it was a member of his family who was involved in this raid, but seeing someone I knew in that situation was a very interesting experience for me. I am not sure what happened to the boy after that.

While I was mayor I drove the black Pontiac station wagon that my predecessor, Gordon Payrow, drove when he was mayor. It was equipped with a siren. I was never sure why Gordon had a siren in his car, but I kind of liked the idea. When I would go to talk to kids, I would let the siren go off so that they could hear it, and it was always a thrill. I used it on several occasions when I was driving out Center Street and another driver would go flying by me, crossing over the double line in the "no passing" zone. I would turn on my siren and pull them over. Bob Galle, the police commissioner, was really upset with me for stopping

---

[1] In 1987 I established a program to have bulletproof vests donated to the police department. Today, it is required that all police officers wear a bulletproof vest, and each officer has one.

left to right: Adam Team Captain Andrew Sotak, Chris Fulmer, Officer Richard Magan

people. He said, "Don't stop anyone in your mayor's car. You never know when some crazy guy might pull out a gun and shoot you." So I stopped doing it on the police commissioner's request.

However, there were two other times I used it. The first had to do with kids on bicycles who ignored stop signs and went right through them into traffic. I stopped one young man, probably in junior high, whose father was very angry that I stopped his kid, because his son was really upset. That was my objective: to upset him, to let him know that as a bicyclist, he was responsible for obeying the rules of the road, and that stopping at stop signs was one of those rules, even for bicycles.

The other time I used it for fun, although it was a serious matter as well, was when I was on Route 22 on my way to Harrisburg. Bob Rudas, the city's solicitor, was in his car in front me, and he was really exceeding the speed limit. There was no one else around, and I thought, "This is my chance to scare him." So I hit the siren. I understand that he almost had a heart attack; he was completely shaken by the siren, and he was sure he had just been caught speeding. But he did slow down for the rest of the trip. Needless to say, I did not press charges.

One recurring problem that the police had was the traffic on Wyandotte Street hill. I believe Wyandotte Street hill has always been a problem, winding its way down South Mountain into the South Side of Bethlehem, and it continues to be one to this very day. There was a man by the name of Toby Clauser; he was one of those citizens who really was concerned about this problem. He lived on the hill, and he called the mayor's office and other departments almost every day, telling us about the trucks that were speeding and the problems with traffic.

Toby wanted me to come meet with him, and one day I decided that I was going to go up and talk with him. Dan Church, a reporter for the *Globe-Times*, heard the news. He had talked to Toby, and Toby was so angry, he said he was going to hit me right in the face with his fist. Dan decided to bring a camera with him so he could get a picture of Toby Clauser hitting the mayor, a photo opportunity which did not impress me much. But I went to see Toby and I listened to what he had to say. He did not hit me, but I am not sure how much we could help him. The city put in speed limit signs and we stationed police on Wyandotte Street hill, but when the police were not there drivers continued to speed.

South Side restaurant owner John Moralis *center* talks with Sgt. Gerald Fox *left* and Charlie Team Captain Joseph Moyer

We had another problem at the bottom of the Wyandotte Street hill, where there was an adult book store. Since it was the first thing that a lot of people saw when they reached the bottom of the hill, that was what welcomed them to the community. Many neighbors called and complained about it, so I said to Bob Galle, "Let's go down and check it out." Bob and I went in the book store to see what kind of books they had, and indeed, there was no question. It was definitely pornographic, not a very welcoming experience to people arriving in the community.

I did hope at the time that there would be no one around with a camera, to take a picture of Police Commissioner Bob Galle and Mayor Gordon Mowrer entering this adult book store. I wondered whether they would try to blackmail us or spread stories that we were frequenting this particular facility. Fortunately no one had a camera, and we were not "frequenting" the establishment. I think that was the only time either of us ever went inside.

Today when you get to the bottom of Wyandotte Street hill, you are greeted in a much more friendly way, by a McDonald's.

One Halloween during my term as mayor, I dressed up in a gorilla suit and walked through City Hall handing out candy corn. I went from department to department handing out the candy corn, having a great time, knowing that no one knew who I was. I went to all the departments to try to cover everyone. I even went to my own office, where my secretary had no idea who I was, and neither did Pat Kesling, who was my administrative assistant.

But the most interesting department that I went to was the police department. I intentionally went to the communications bureau, which really was the heart of the police operations, to see how they would respond. Someone going there with the wrong intentions could destroy everything that was going on in the city, because all the emergency phone calls and all the dispatches went

Stanley Zweifel, deputy police commissioner, in the Communications Control Center at City Hall

through that office. I went in and gave out the candy, and nobody challenged me, nobody questioned me, no one knew who I was.

Later that day, after I had changed my clothes, I went to a staff meeting. I asked if anybody knew who the gorilla who went through City Hall handing out candy corn was,

left to right: Walter W. Keyes, Baker Team Captain John Yerk, Detective Douglas Groenewald, and an unidentified officer

and they all said no. I announced that it was me. They all looked shocked. I told them that I was most disturbed by how gullible our police department was, and how open it was to potential problems, because I had proven that anybody could walk in there and potentially cause a serious problem. After that, the police began to be more aware of security, developing plans to keep non-official people from going in and becoming stricter about accessibility. All that was because a gorilla went through City Hall at Halloween.

When I was mayor, it was my policy that if I got a traffic ticket, I was going to pay it. Anybody else who got a ticket and asked me to take care of it for them would have to understand that since I paid for my own ticket, they would have to pay for their own tickets. I believe there might have been one or two occasions when someone was so angry at getting a ticket, and had been a great supporter of mine, that I said, "Give me the ticket, I'll pay it." I paid those tickets myself, I did not "fix" them. I paid maybe one or two tickets in all the time I was mayor. I know in the past there were mayors who did take care of tickets for people, but my philosophy was, "If you did it, you have to pay for it." That even included my wife; you will read her story later.

During my term as mayor, I was part of the Governor's Justice Commission, which would meet once a month. For the most part, the Governor's Justice Commission approved proposals for financing projects to reduce crime within the community. Often we would meet in Harrisburg, and sometimes in Wilkes-Barre. As a result of this I got to visit a number of work sites for juvenile offenders, because I was involved with that division.

When I went to one of these "camps," we would often have lunch with some of the residents. I remember meeting with a young man, having lunch with him, and asking why he was there. He replied, "I was breaking windows, doing vandalism." I asked him if he liked to break windows. "Yes," he replied, "It's great fun." So I said, "When you get out of here, you come to Bethlehem, and come up to the mayor's office. Tell the secretary that you're the one that I had lunch with at Rutherford, and you want to see me." I continued, "You and I together will go to one of the buildings that is going to be torn down for redevelopment, and we will both get rocks and break every window in the place. What do you think of that?" And he said to me, "That doesn't sound like fun." Seeing the difference in his reaction to doing something when it was forbidden and when it was permitted was quite informative.

One quality that I always recognized about the police department was the pride that the officers took in their work. I was very impressed with the police officers, their attitude toward the city, their attitude toward citizens, and their willingness to do their part to make Bethlehem a better place in which to live. Bethlehem has always had an excellent police department, with police officers who really care about our community. We have been truly blessed, and it appears that the blessing continues.

Chapter

6

Always Improving: The Fire Department

I remember Penn Elementary School and my first four teachers. I remember many of the students who were in my class, for many of them graduated from Liberty High School with me. I remember a lot of things about growing up – but especially I remember that next to Penn School was the Fairview Fire Station. As a child, I remember walking by the fire house, looking in at the big red fire engine and watching the firemen play cards, talk about baseball, and wash their cars. There was excitement when the fire sirens went off and the fire trucks would go racing down the street. Never did I imagine that someday the firefighters of Bethlehem would work under my direction, or that at times I would wear a fire helmet and uniform to fires in Bethlehem.

Back then, I wondered what firefighters did when they were not fighting fires. Sometimes I wondered the same thing when I became mayor. So in my usual style of leadership, I decided to stop in unannounced one day and see what went on. I learned that not much had changed since I was a boy, as I watched one of the men washing his car. I discovered that he saw nothing wrong with that – as long as there was no fire at the time, why not?

When I told this story to my grandchildren, one of them agreed that this was acceptable. The old view was that a firefighter had to be ready to fight a fire at a moment's notice. When there was no fire, the job of a firefighter was to wait for one, and passing the time with tasks that were not job-related was acceptable. After all, you can only wash the fire engines and check equipment so much.

Because of my background in management, and my experience in business, I had a whole new philosophy. My guide was "an ounce of prevention is worth a pound of cure." It was obviously important to check equipment regularly to be sure it was in excellent and ready order, and they did that. But there was much more that could be done. There had been an alarming number of incidents of arson and house fires during the fall of 1973 in Bethlehem. We needed to focus on how to prevent fires and cut losses.

Almost immediately after I began my term as mayor in 1974, I divided the Department of Public Safety into two separate departments, one for fire and one for police. Instead of a Fire Chief, I named a new Fire Commissioner, who reported directly to me. I met with the new Fire Commissioner, Joseph Trilli, and the Deputy Commissioner, Augustine Sebastionelli, and we began to put together a plan. They recognized the importance of training and liked the "management by objectives" principles that I was beginning to instill.

We had numerous sessions to discuss the results that we wanted, and how we could put together obtainable goals that could be quantified. The officers themselves developed their objectives with the help of some consultants from Penn State University, who were advising the city on how to incorporate the "management by objectives" principles.

Fire Commissioner Joseph Trilli *right* and Deputy Commissioner
Augustine Sebastionelli *Courtesy the Express-Times*

They put together a systematic plan for the fire department
which involved all the firefighters in the decision-making
process.

These new goals included housing and commercial inspections. For a housing inspection, the inspectors went directly to a house, at the request of the owner and with the owner's permission, and physically walked through the property. The inspectors would point out possible fire hazards to the owner. Sometimes there were numerous issues which needed to be addressed in order to prevent potential fires. Often these inspections happened in the evening when the owners were home from work.

The pre-fire planning and in-service inspections were much more detailed for commercial buildings. They took place more often during the day when the businesses were in operation. The inspectors wanted to know where the fire hydrants were located, what kind of fire they might be fighting, and what problems they might have in fighting a fire. If the firefighters had walked through the business with the workers, they would understand what they might be getting into if a fire broke out, and they would be better able to prevent the spread of the fire. Having an understanding of who might be in the building at the time of a fire would be helpful in projecting what injuries or issues the firefighters would be facing. The more information the firefighters had, the better able they were to fight a fire.

Change was one of the themes of my administration, and it was no different with the dress of the firefighters. In February, 1975, we did away with the formal uniforms and adopted burgundy blazers and royal blue slacks. We thought that the more casual uniforms would make the firefighters seem less authoritarian, and perhaps people would accept them more easily when they came for an inspection. The men seemed to enjoy them. Those were the days before there were women firefighters.

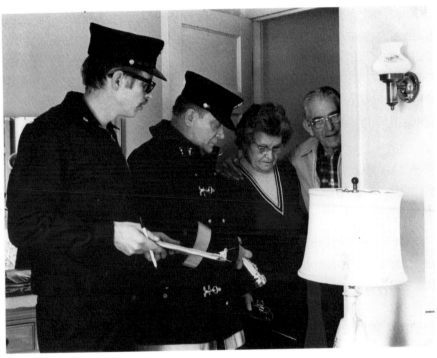

Firefighters Gary Briggs and Linford Hillegas discuss fire hazards with Mr. and Mrs. William Smith on a home inspection.

You never know when a major fire will occur. The worst fire Bethlehem ever had, until that point, was in October, 1974, at Burron Medical Products, located on Twelfth Avenue. The company was a major manufacturer of plastic medical equipment, employing about 400 people. Plastic burns very hot and very fast, and the city was soon covered with a cloud of sooty black smoke. As a result of that fire, we learned the fire department needed more gas masks. I personally took some of our men to St. Luke's Hospital to be checked out, some for breathing problems and some because exposure to the chemicals in the smoke caused them to develop an itchy rash.

The plant had no sprinkler or fire suppression system – a lot of factories did not have them in those days – but it was equipped with what Burron's vice president for operations called "the most modern fire alarm system devised," using heat and smoke sensors which sent alarms directly to the city's communications center.[1] Despite that, damages were estimated to be almost three million dollars. The fire was eventually determined to have been caused by arson.

The company's owners and employees were back on site the next day, and back in business after a few weeks. Burron was once again a thriving business within months. The Burron company was purchased by B. Braun in 1979.

Another major fire hit Bethlehem in February,1977 as eighteen shops in the Westgate Mall were damaged in an early morning fire. I spent a great deal of time at the fire and again took some firefighters to St. Luke's to have them checked. Westgate had been built before automatic sprinklers were required, and the damages exceeded three million dollars. That fire, too, was eventually determined to be caused by arson.

There are some questions which have remained unanswered concerning the fire, which spread through the space just under the roof. The fire officials claimed that the builder did not install the appropriate fire walls. The builder claimed that he did. The state came in and examined the debris after the fire, but they never came to a conclusion.

I had the opportunity to walk through Hess's,[2] one of the stores that was damaged, with Phil Berman, who was

[1]"Records Saved in Burron Fire," Mary Wagner, *Bethlehem Globe-Times*, October 22, 1974, p. 17.

[2]Philip Berman bought the company, which had several locations, from Max Hess in 1968. Two years after the Westgate fire, in October 1979, he sold the expanded company to Crown American. The Hess's name was retired in 1994 when many of the stores were purchased by Bon Ton.

During the Westgate fire, I consulted for a moment with Deputy
Commissioner Augustine Sebastionelli *left*. From the look of the gear,
you can tell which is the firefighter and which is the mayor!

After the Westgate fire, a representative of Hess's *left* presented a check for $1,000 for the firefighters' pension fund to me, Fire Commissioner Joe Trilli *right*, and a representative of the firefighters' union.

the owner at the time, to assess the damages. Hess's was very appreciative of the fire department's help and later presented the city with a check for $1,000 for the Fire Pension fund.

A continuing problem for the firefighters was some Lehigh University students. The university was not always a wonderful neighbor. The students on the hill would set off fire alarm boxes with false alarms during the night. One night at the end of April, 1975, someone sent two false alarms from alarm boxes located close to two fraternity houses. As the fire trucks approached, students greeted them by throwing stones and bricks, damaging one fire truck and hitting at least one firefighter. The students also surrounded the truck when it stopped and refused to let it pass.

At the next MBO session we talked about what we might do. One of the men suggested we remove the fire alarm boxes. We decided that would be a good solution. Students could phone in a fire, if there was one, and we would be able to trace the phone from which the call was made if the call was not legitimate. The next year, we removed many more fire alarm boxes from locations in the city, and the number of false alarms dropped considerably.

In early January of 1976, the Christmas tree on the Hill-to-Hill Bridge was set on fire. It was the most recognizable symbol of Christmas in Bethlehem after the lighted star on South Mountain. Nearby, inspectors found a discarded can which had contained gasoline. They ruled out an electrical cause because power to all city Christmas lights, including the tree, had been disconnected earlier in the day. The Hill-to-Hill tree had also been set on fire in 1971, and in 1950 three Lehigh students were fined and suspended for setting a tree in the same location on fire. Although there were rumors and jokes about who might be responsible, the arsonist was never identified.

In early 1975, a movie about a catastrophic fire in a high-rise building, *The Towering Inferno*, was released, and caused concern in the Bethlehem community about fire safety in the city's high-rise buildings. Most had no sprinkler systems, and the fire department had only a 100-foot ladder truck, which meant that residents on the eleventh floor and above could not be reached from outside the building. Several high-rise buildings to house senior citizens were being planned at the time, and more tall

My administration placed great importance on keeping the fire equipment up to date, including purchasing a new fire truck in 1976.

buildings were expected to be developed. It was a timely issue.

I recently asked Commissioner Trilli what he thought the greatest accomplishment of his department was during our time of leadership. Without a doubt, he said, it was getting an ordinance passed which required automatic sprinklers in any new building taller than sixty feet. This was a very controversial issue. The fire department was in favor of the bill, which it felt would save lives in the event of a fire in a tall residential or office building. Others, led by architects and developers, felt that the added cost for sprinklers would encourage developers to move proposed projects from Bethlehem to locations which had fewer requirements. After several months of deliberations and publicity, the ordinance was passed in September, 1975. Bethlehem became the first city in the Lehigh Valley to pass such an ordinance.

Several years after I left office, the *Morning Call* printed an article with the headline, "Fire proves sprinkler ordinance right." Five years after the ordinance was passed, Bethlehem had a fire in a high-rise building, the Fred B. Rooney Building on the South Side. The sprinklers worked and saved the life of a resident. The article began, "Paul Calvo, Dolores Caskey and Joseph Trilli have to feel especially satisfied with themselves these days."[3] Needless to say, I do, too!

Firefighters are prepared to risk their lives every day in the service of their community. They handle not only fires, hazardous materials, and other life-threatening situations, but also issues of fire safety and prevention, education, and whatever needs to be done to make Bethlehem a better, safer place to live. I am very proud of the positive changes to the department and the accomplishments of the men and their leadership during my time as mayor.

---

[3]"Fire proves sprinkler ordinance right, proponents say," Tom Schroeder, the *Morning Call*, April 23, 1980, p. 85.

Chapter

7

Celebrating the Bicentennial

I still consider it rather extraordinary that I was the mayor of Bethlehem in 1976 during the American Bicentennial year, which celebrated the 200th anniversary of America's independence. It was a moment when we marked 200 years of challenge and change, hope and hurt, and yesterdays and todays. But most important, it was the celebration of 200 years of millions of people grasping to understand the meaning of the idea "that all men are created equal, that they are endowed by their Creator with certain unalienable rights, that among these are life, liberty, and the pursuit of happiness." It was an idea to be tested and developed during that period, one which continues to be tested and developed in our generation today.

It was with this in mind that I needed to find someone to be the Bicentennial coordinator for all the activities that Bethlehem might be responsible for during that year. I had known Anne McGeady for many years. She was a very active citizen, born and raised in Bethlehem, and she had participated in many activities. I thought she would be an outstanding person to be the coordinator, and so I selected her. A number of people were unhappy with my selection because she happened to be a Republican and I was a Democrat. However, that's politics.

She was responsible for coordinating many areas, including numerous celebrations by various ethnic groups whose immigrants have come to the United States. Among these were the Slovaks, the Greeks, the Italians, the Polish, the Puerto Ricans, the Portuguese, the Ukrainians, the Jewish people, and many more. All of these nationalities wanted to celebrate the country's great birthday and what it came to represent.

Bethlehem's Bicentennial celebration began with a musical concert in Liberty High School's auditorium, conducted by Dr. John Raymond, director of the college choir and glee club of Lafayette College. Members of all the church choirs participated. Tom Morgan made all the arrangements. It was a delightful evening.

The Goodfellows organization of Bethlehem was responsible for bringing the Tamburitzans from Duquesne University to Bethlehem. Their ethnic dress, music and dance represented some of the eastern European countries which had played an important role in Bethlehem's history and culture. It was very colorful and marvelous, and many people in Bethlehem were able to enjoy the color and culture that was alive that night during the concert.

Bethlehem had the honor of being one of the stops for the American Freedom Train, which came with all kinds of memorabilia of the first 200 years of America. It was an actual steam-powered train, which included twelve cars with exhibits and displays from American history. It was one of the only national celebrations of the nation's Bicentennial, and over a period of twenty-one months it visited all forty-eight contiguous states.

I asked Anne McGeady how the Freedom Train happened to come to Bethlehem. She said that Kate Laepple,

Officials drove a spike into the railroad tracks in preparation for the Freedom Train to come to town.

One of the benefits of being mayor: acting as engineer for the Freedom Train.

My children enjoyed seeing the Freedom Train with me.

who worked in the Morning Call office in Bethlehem, came to her and said, "I have some information for you if you want it, but if I give it to you and you are successful, you must give me the first write-up on this so I can publish it in the *Morning Call.*" Anne agreed.

In those days there was a great deal of competition between the *Morning Call* in Allentown and the *Bethlehem Globe-Times* (now the *Express-Times*). Each wanted to have the scoop on what the activity was, so that their paper could publish it first. This is one of the cases where the first dibs went to the *Morning Call*, because Kate advised Anne that the Freedom Train was available through this connection. Anne made the contact, and the Freedom Train was signed up, and therefore the *Morning Call* got the story.

The August day the Freedom Train came to town was exciting because the committee, elected officials, and key people were invited to go outside of Bethlehem, get on the Freedom Train and ride into Bethlehem. Before we did this, we drove in a ceremonial spike to prepare for the train. We rode the train, which was exciting, and had a roast beef dinner, which was wonderfully delicious.

Thousands of people lined up to see the exhibits of memorabilia and art on the train as it stood on the tracks at the city. I remember that there were a lot of paintings. Besides that, there were over five hundred very special artifacts on the train, including George Washington's copy of the U.S. Constitution, a replica of the Liberty Bell called the "Freedom Bell," the original Louisiana Purchase document, items representing many of the ethnic groups that contributed to the culture of the United States, Bing Crosby's gold record of "White Christmas," Joe Frazier's boxing trunks, Arnold Palmer's Masters trophy, Martin

When the Freedom Train came to Bethlehem, crowds gathered, people came; it was a big success.

Luther King's pulpit and robes, and even a rock from the moon. During the three days the Freedom Train was in Bethlehem, about 40,000 people saw the exhibits.

Another activity was the Liberty Bell Trek, which followed the route of the Liberty Bell on its flight for safe-keeping in September, 1777, during the Revolutionary War. The re-enacted trek came to Bethlehem the week of September 19th, retracing the Liberty Bell's journey from Christ Church in Philadelphia, where it began, all the way to Allentown, where it ended. Bethlehem was conveniently the second to the last stop.

The trek caravan was composed of fourteen wagons carrying bells, the Liberty Bell wagon carrying a full-sized replica of the Liberty Bell, and about 140 additional wagons with military scouts, all wearing appropriate costumes. It was a beautiful day as they arrived in Bethlehem on Main Street. The background of downtown Bethlehem, especially Main Street, Hotel Bethlehem and that entire scenic view, was particularly appropriate.

The Freedom High School Fife and Drum Corps escorted the caravan. The Liberty Bell model, which was on one of the horse-drawn wagons, made its way past the Hotel Bethlehem to the Single Brethren's House, where a ceremony was held. There was also an opportunity for people to sign the Declaration of Independence. It was fascinating to watch people sign the document.

To me, one of the things that most stood out during the year was our Night at the City Center, held on July 10. We had learned that there was a German band playing at a ten-day festival in Barnesville. We made contact through Bob Steinmetz and Gus Skrivanek to find out whether they could come to Bethlehem for a night, so that we might be

The Liberty Bell Trek arriving in Bethlehem

Mayor Mowrer signing the Declaration of Independence

able to have a party on the plaza and serve beer. Jeff Parks first got involved with Bethlehem festivities at this time, and thought this was a great idea. He and Kate Laepple and numerous other people got involved and made the contacts. The band agreed to come, and we agreed to allow them to have beer on the plaza.

The night of the party, the festivities were to start at 7 o'clock. We anticipated that about 500 people might come out. We had *5,000* come out! Within half an hour, we ran out of beer. We sent out everybody on the committee and anybody else we could find – Bucky Szulborski, Kate Laepple, Anne and Mac McGeady, Jeff Parks – to some of the local beer companies and some of the bars, to see if we could get more beer, so that we would have enough. The band played the German music, the people celebrated, and it was an absolutely fantastic evening. I even got to direct the band. I also walked around the plaza taping a radio program for WGPA. Everyone I spoke with thought it was a marvelous event. They were right.

Jeff Parks picked up on the idea that this was something Bethlehem had that we should develop. Jeff went on to found and become president of ArtsQuest, the organization responsible for Musikfest, Christkindlmarkt, and other major Bethlehem events. The seeds were planted in 1976 for Musikfest, later to be developed and supported by Mayor Marcincin. Frank Banko was another of the early supporters, who later helped Jeff start Musikfest. It wasn't Musikfest in 1976, but it turned out to be a musikfest. I celebrate that, birthed during the Bicentennial year. I think it has made a big difference in Bethlehem.

Many other things happened during the Bicentennial year, including the flag-raising ceremony, where we brought in the children from Sayre Child Center to hang

Gordon with the director of the German band

I got to direct the German band during the night on the plaza.

Children from Sayre Child Center with the Bicentennial flag

the flag; we had fire hydrants painted in patriotic themes; we had a contest where people painted pictures and the winning pictures were sold in the local bookstores; there were poetry contests for children, and other contests.

The final day of the official celebration, July 4th, was a particularly wonderful climax. We opened the day at the City Center plaza with a Festival of Faith and Freedom, an ecumenical service, which began at 8:30 a.m. But people started coming to the service very early in the morning. Anne McGeady claims that people were walking down to

Winners of the Bicentennial Drawing Contest	
1. Fred Bees	*Old Moravian Chapel* View from Central Church Lawn
2. Howard Breisch	*Lehigh Canal Activity* Vicinity of Old New Street Bridge
3. Joe Charnoski	*Kemerer Museum*
4. Joe Charnoski	*Packer Memorial Chapel*
5. Jane W. Conneen	*The Nain House* Heckewelder Place
6. Monica J. Dietrich	*Market Street East*
7. Diane Dow	*Illick's Mill* Monocacy Park
8. Viola Kravits	*The Last Trolley*
9. Debby Persall	*Moravian Sisters Home* West Church Street, South Campus
10. Mario Rossetti	*The Bell House*
11. Betsy Coupe Tinsman	*Old Bethlehem Waterworks*
12. Arthur F. Weiss	*Bethlehem's N. J. Central Station*

the plaza while she was still sleeping; she heard them from her room as some of them were carrying chairs, making some noise in preparation for the service. The plaza was packed with people from all faiths and all backgrounds, as we celebrated the service. One count said that 5,000 people attended the event.

Later during the day there was a big parade that included all of the different community representatives and elected officials. Congressman Fred B. Rooney participated in the

On July 4, local actor Humphrey Fry led the procession of local officials. Congressman Fred B. Rooney and I were first, followed by members of the Bethlehem City Council.

activity, Humphrey Fry led the service and ceremonies in appropriate Colonial attire, and there were opportunities for people to sign the Declaration of Independence, which was read at the affair.

We completed the celebration with a big birthday party. This particular birthday party ended like all others, with a giant birthday cake. Following this fantastically-tasting birthday cake, we had quite a creative display of fireworks for all to see. Overall I felt that the entire Bicentennial year had gone by smoothly. The people seemed very enthusiastic, and very happy to have had this great opportunity.

One of the fire hydrants which was painted as part of the celebration

Chapter

8

Bethlehem's Sister Cities: Engaging the World

Bethlehem owes a great deal to the immigrants from other countries who have made this city what it is. From the original founders of the city who came from Germany, Moravia and Bohemia, and England, to the steelworkers and their families who came from many countries and ethnicities in Europe, to the more recent influx of people from Puerto Rico and Mexico, Asia, and other locations, each new group has added to the rich culture and lifestyle which we enjoy in Bethlehem today. It is fitting that Bethlehem celebrates that international flavor by maintaining relationships with three Sister Cities: Tondabayashi, Japan; Schwäbisch Gmünd, Germany; and Murska Sobota, Slovenia.

The idea of two cities establishing a mutual relationship was an aftermath of World War II. Some American cities sent relief supplies to locations in Europe, and cities from other countries "adopted" cities which had suffered in the war. In the 1950s President Eisenhower established a forerunner of the sister city movement to promote peace by encouraging individuals to work together in order to learn about each other. In 1967, Sister Cities International (SCI) was founded to encourage partnerships between U.S. cities and international communities. Its mission is "to promote peace through mutual respect, understanding and cooperation – one individual, one community at a time." As a nonprofit citizen diplomacy network, it strives "to build global cooperation at the municipal level, promote cultural understanding and stimulate economic development."

Even before the founding of Sister Cities International, Bethlehem had begun a relationship with Tondabayashi, Japan, the result of a friendship developed by a former resident of Bethlehem whose job transferred him to Japan. In addition, both cities were known as "The Christmas City" in their respective countries. One of Tondabayashi's major industries produced glass Christmas ornaments, and Bethlehem used many of those products.

In the mid-1960s, an unofficial "sister city committee" was founded in Bethlehem. City Council officially established a Sister City Commission of the City of Bethlehem in November, 1972. Its purpose was "to promote friendship and understanding between Bethlehem and Tondabayashi, to exchange cultural interests, to promote trade interests and tourism, and to oversee a Student Exchange Program between Bethlehem and its Japanese sister city of Tondabayashi." I was a member of City Council when this issue was presented.

One of the tangible results of the relationship between the two cities was the donation of a Japanese garden to the City of Bethlehem in 1971. A well-known landscape architect from Tondabayashi, Yoshinaga Sakon, presented the garden as a gift to his Sister City. The "Garden of Serenity" was planted next to the new Bethlehem Area Public Library.

In 1974, as I was beginning my first term as mayor, Mr. Sakon returned to Bethlehem bringing a Japanese

The Garden of Serenity

teahouse which he had commissioned for the Japanese garden. He had ordered it built in Japan by an expert carpenter. The teahouse was then deconstructed, every piece was numbered, and the pieces were packed to be shipped to Bethlehem. The teahouse was reassembled with the help of some city workers during the summer.

After the teahouse was reassembled, it still needed a proper roof, since a roof would have been too heavy to ship. We wanted to comply with Mr. Sakon's request that the roof be made of copper, which would make it authentic. We tried to find money for a copper roof, but were having some difficulty, when New Jersey Zinc came forward and offered to put a zinc roof on the teahouse for free. Some

Putting together the Japanese teahouse *left to right:* landscape architects Hashiro Tanaka and Yoshinaga Sakon, Bethlehem parks director Joseph Mangan, the mayor of Tondabayashi and me. *Courtesy the Express-Times*

Two of the principal workers from Bethlehem who assembled the teahouse were Paul Hassick, *second from left* and Charlie Brown *right.* The others in this photo are Yuichi Fukuhara, the interpreter, landscape architect Hashiro Tanaka, and the mayors of Bethlehem and Tondabayashi. *Courtesy the Express-Times*

of us thought that was a great idea, but Mr. Sakon said zinc was not authentic, and he wanted a copper roof. Lehigh Engineering, Inc. eventually agreed to provide an authentic copper roof for the teahouse.

For the dedication of the teahouse in August, 1975, we had a packed place. Larry Fenninger, who was part of Bethlehem Steel at the time, was instrumental in making it a success. He and Bernie Cohen worked hard to make it a very exciting event. People came from everywhere, the crowd was heavy, and it was fun. Special tea ceremonies were performed for the public, and people got a better understanding of Japan. Mr. Sakon came for the dedication, and rearranged some of the garden. To this day, it is an absolutely beautiful, very serene kind of place.

There have been many functions that have been held at the teahouse, including special tea ceremonies. It is a favorite spot for weddings; periodically I drive by on a weekend, and see a couple dressed formally, with a group around them as they celebrate their wedding vows.

The mayor of Tondabayashi, Kiyoshi Nishioka, and I exchanged visits to each others' cities for several years. He spoke about as much English as I spoke Japanese (which was not very much), but we both enjoyed the experiences. When the mayor of Tondabayashi was in Bethlehem, we had a young man named Yuichi Fukuhara, a Lehigh student, act as an interpreter. His father was the president of Shiseido Cosmetics, which I believe was the second largest cosmetics company in the world at the time, and his son was a very good interpreter.

The mayor of Tondabayashi's first visit was in the summer of 1974, when he accompanied Mr. Sakon and the pieces of the teahouse. For that occasion, the mayor

Larry Fenninger led the official dedication of the Garden of Serenity, as a large crowd watched.

visited with my family and actually stayed in our house. The mayor was wonderful. Whenever he would speak, he said it was so wonderful to be here in this "Sister Shitty." And of course, every time he said that, people responded with laughter. On the Fourth of July he was beaming as he watched the fireworks, thinking that all this was done in celebration of his coming to the Lehigh Valley.

In 1975, my wife, my twelve-year-old son, my young daughter, who was nine at the time, and I all decided to go visit Tondabayashi. (Our youngest daughter, Meg, was about two, so she stayed in Bethlehem with my brother and his wife.) We flew to Tokyo, where we were welcomed to Japan by the president of Shiseido Cosmetics, who was very happy that we had involved his son in our community. He took Mary and myself and our two children out to probably one of the swankiest restaurants in all of Tokyo, and it was not a cheap night! In fact, his company, Shiseido

Cosmetics, arranged for exclusive use of the restaurant for that evening, and we were entertained royally. I even had a young geisha come up and say that she was available for any services I might need. Of course, she said it right in front of my wife; it was kind of an interesting experience for me, but I was unsure what to say or do.

When we got to Tondabayashi, which is about three hundred miles southwest of Tokyo in the Osaka area, we were greeted by a number of the people from the town. The mayor was there, with his car and driver, and I rode in the mayor's car with him, the driver and an interpreter. The second car was the mayor's wife, my wife and an interpreter. Then there were several cars that had the councilmen from the city. In the last car were my two children, with some people who spoke no English and with no interpreter. When we got to the first stop, my son and daughter came running up and said, "Don't leave us alone with them! We don't know what they are saying!"

I learned as a result of my trip that the Japanese people are about as hospitable as anyone can be. If I said I need some film, the next thing I knew, I had six or eight packs of film on my desk. If I said I like lobster, all of a sudden we were having the most delicious lobster we ever imagined. It seemed that no request was too much.

In Tondabayashi there is a very modern structure called the Perfect Liberty Peace Tower, built as a headquarters for a new religion called Perfect Liberty. We got to go up in the tower and we got to eat in the tower. We were just treated fantastically.

The Japanese people had heard that I like wrestling, and once wrestled in college. At the time that we were there, the national sumo wrestling championship was

Our family was welcomed to Japan by Mr. Sakon.

The mayors of Tondabayashi and Bethlehem with their families

taking place, and they got tickets for the four of us to go. It was one of the most incredible experiences of my life. We sat in a little square area flat on the floor, and we looked out over the area where the men were wrestling. They were *big* men. At the end of the match, when the champion was declared, everybody took the cushion that they were sitting on and threw it down to the wrestling area, so that there was a snowstorm of pillows that hit the two sumo wrestling champions. It was really exciting – not quite as exciting as Grace Hall and Lehigh, but still exciting.

The Sister City relationship between Bethlehem and Schwäbisch Gmünd, Germany, was formalized in 1991, but the process began six years earlier. I have had several opportunities to visit Schwäbisch Gmünd. In 1987 when I was mayor the second time, I went with Jeff Parks and a group from Bethlehem to review the Christkindlmarkt and get ideas to bring back to Bethlehem.

I was overwhelmed by the fellowship and the friendship shown by the people from Schwäbisch Gmünd. Dr. Robert Marcincin of Bethlehem, who is a friend and who did some surgery on my back, had a connection with a doctor in Schwäbisch Gmünd who specialized in unusual foot operations. I was having some problems at the time, and he hoped that the doctor could help. He introduced me to the doctor, and while I was there I went with Jeff Parks to have a consultation.

Later in 1987 I went back for surgery. As a courtesy to the Sister City program, my hospital stay was entirely free. There was no charge to me, the surgeon did not charge anything for his operation, and they even got a room in a lovely hotel for my wife, and there was no charge for that. An interesting sidelight is they gave her a bouquet of flowers which was absolutely gorgeous. Unfortunately, she had an allergy to the flowers, and had a terrible time breathing.

The relationship between the two cities has been very fruitful, providing the inspiration for Bethlehem's Musikfest in the summer and Christkindlmarkt in December. I remember the official celebration establishing the Sister City partnership, when Dr. Wolfgang Schuster, Lord Mayor of Schwäbisch Gmünd, and his wife came over to the United States. Although Ken Smith was mayor of Bethlehem at the time, Mary and I also participated in some of the events with the Schusters. We have since had the opportunity to see them come back several times.

I have not had the pleasure of visiting Bethlehem's third Sister City, Murska Sobota, Slovenia, which joined the other two Sister Cities in 1996. However, as a member of City Council, I have helped to raise their flag on Slovenia Day in Bethlehem.

When we were in Japan, almost all Japanese students wanted to come to the United States to study. Their goal in life was to study abroad and to get an American education. Many people came up to us and asked how they could get scholarships and how they could come to the United States. So it is fitting that perhaps the most important thing that has emerged from the Sister City program is the youth exchange. Each year, Bethlehem sends young people to their countries, or they send young people to our country. There have been many wonderful exchanges and long-term relationships established from these visits.

The hospitality of both the Sister Cities which I have visited is absolutely fantastic. The program certainly does promote positive relationships and good feelings between our cities here in the United States and their Sister Cities throughout the world.

Chapter

9

More Building

Even though I think that the most significant undertaking of my years as mayor was the redevelopment of the downtown, there were many other municipal building projects undertaken by my administration. They may not have attracted the attention that the Main Street project and the completion of the First Valley Bank plaza and skating rink did, but they were important for Bethlehem's development nevertheless. I sometimes referred to these as "quality of life" projects.

One of the first areas to benefit during my administration was Bethlehem's South Side, which had been neglected by city government for many years. In 1974, we began a housing rehabilitation program, which provided low interest loans as well as some outright grants to improve housing in that part of town. We got the vo-tech school involved, and the students helped to rehabilitate many houses. We also allocated some city funds to improve streets, plant trees, and work on developing a new central business district in the area of Fourth Street.

One of my roles as mayor was to make contacts for state and federal funding which could benefit Bethlehem. Much of the money needed for the South Side improvements came from community development funds, a new program

We placed a lot of emphasis on rehabilitating homes.

signed into law by the federal government in 1974. We knew that this program was in the works, and put together an application for funds with the help of individual citizens, members of City Council, and staff from my administration. As soon as President Ford signed the enabling legislation, we were able to submit our application to the state, which redistributed the funds from the federal government. In fact, Bethlehem was the first city in Pennsylvania to apply for these funds, and Bethlehem received a Community Development Block Grant (CDBG) of over $1.2 million as a result.

In October, 1976, Pennsylvania Governor Milton J. Shapp visited Bethlehem, and I interviewed him on my

WGPA radio program. One of the topics we discussed was the housing grant. Governor Shapp stated:

> "We get proposals from various cities on housing . . . the proposal that Bethlehem submitted for housing was superior to some of the other proposals that were submitted. And so we utilized the funding that we got through the Department of Community Affairs, and accepted the Bethlehem proposal, whereas other communities that have not done what you've done, really, put together all the facilities in your community to work on this thing and got the right agencies, they get less from the state. Some of that is competitive, but it's your own work, not ours."

Reese Jones was one of the movers and shakers of my time as mayor. He was very active in Gordon Payrow's time as well. He was president of First Valley Bank, and in those days that was the bank that was most influential in the downtown.[1] Reese was very cooperative and he wanted to see Bethlehem move forward. The ice skating rink downtown as a miniature Rockefeller Center rink was his vision. He wanted more than anything to build high-rise buildings downtown. He went around and talked to a number of churches to try to get them to build senior citizen high-rises, so that at least there would be the appearance that something was going on with new buildings in our downtown area. His efforts were successful. By the end of 1977, ground had been broken for three different senior citizen high-rise buildings: Moravian House II on Main Street (the first Moravian House high-rise was completed in 1974), Lutheran Manor at Westgate Drive, and the South Side high-rise at Fourth and New Streets.

---

[1] Several mergers and name changes later, it is now part of Bank of America.

It was not easy to get these projects going. We were trying to make a major change in people's mind-sets, from tearing down and rebuilding to preserving and rehabilitating what was already there. The community really supported the idea of restoring Main Street. Bethlehem still had to do a certain amount of rebuilding, however, because there were areas, such as the location of the South Side high-rise, that had been cleared by the Bethlehem Redevelopment Authority. We wanted an opportunity to develop those empty sites to fit in with what we were trying to do in other parts of the city, to provide a modern functional building.

Some of the owners of run-down buildings saw an opportunity for a big profit. They wanted the Redevelopment Authority to purchase their property, clear the ground, and put up a new building, all with government money. Because of this idea, we wound up with all kinds of lawsuits, whether it was over the parking garage or clearing land to build senior citizen high-rises, with lots of problems and great difficulties. They slowed down some of the progress, but they were unable to stop it.

In January of 1977, the ground had been cleared for the $4.5 million South Side high-rise, and we had two private developers ready to put up the building, but we still had no commitment for the rest of the money we needed for construction. It looked like the federal money for the project was not going to be available. President Ford and his administration were getting ready to leave Washington, D.C., and it was questionable whether President Carter's incoming administration would continue to fund this project. Hoping to get approval before the inauguration on January 20, I flew down to Washington to meet with the Secretary of Housing and Urban Development (HUD) nominee, Patricia Harris, on January 5. We still received no commitment, so in February we made a twelve-minute movie about the project with my new home-movie camera, which was innovative technology for the time. It was a good movie, homemade but interesting. On February 23 my administrative assistant Dan Fitzpatrick, several staff members and I returned to Washington to show the movie.

I met with Secretary Harris's secretary, and she said Ms. Harris would not be available. I said I was not leaving until I showed this movie, so she arranged for me to meet with one of the Secretary's top aides. He watched the movie, and then he asked what I wanted. I said we needed approval of the funding so that we could proceed with the building. He immediately told me, "You have it." I had been in government long enough that I was skeptical. I told him I did not believe him, and where had he been all this time? He repeated that we would have the money, and that he just had to notify our congressman. I gave him his name and he notified Fred Rooney.

The next day Congressman Rooney called me on the phone and said, "Evidently you have more influence in Washington than I do." We got the money, Section 8 funding which guaranteed HUD supplements for low-income renters, particularly the elderly. I was really thrilled that we were able do it. It was the first major building project on the South Side in many years, and it included housing as well as several stores and commercial space on the first floor. It was intended to be the anchor for a new commercial district on Fourth Street. We named the high-rise after Fred Rooney, and it became known as The Fred B. Rooney Building.

Cutting the rope at the entrance to the canal towpath on the South Side are me, Representative Fred Rooney, Dolores Caskey, and Paul Calvo, watched by local children including George Mowrer at the far right.

We spent a lot of time fixing the canal next to the Lehigh River.

Parks and Recreation was another area that we worked on consistently during my time in office. The first year we began work on two new parks for the South Side, on land donated by the Bethlehem School District. We sought federal funds for an indoor-outdoor swimming pool complex at Broughal Junior High School, although that project was later cancelled when no funds and no citizen interest were forthcoming. We began construction of Westside Park, for which residents had been waiting almost forty years, and a park at the site of the former Higbee School.

By the time I left office at the end of 1977, the Department of Parks and Public Property had created, renovated, or updated almost every City park in Bethlehem. The new nine-hole golf course and driving range at Illick's Mill had been completed and was open for business. The tennis court building at Sand Island was remodeled. The eroding banks of Monocacy Park were repaired, and the Lehigh Canal was restored as a place for nature-lovers to walk or ride.

At the same time that I was trying to promote refurbishing and reusing the buildings on Main Street, I had also inherited the modern building project on Broad Street, a leftover from the Clarke & Rapuano plan. Closing Broad Street, erecting a large office and bank structure, and developing the Bethlehem Plaza Mall for downtown shopping meant that there would be a significant need for parking spaces. The proposed convention center and performing arts theater would also need ample parking. To support all these needs, the City planned to build a parking garage on Walnut Street, behind the Broad Street mall and close to the other projected development.

The City had committed to this project during Gordon Payrow's administration, but it was up to me to complete it.

For the first annual Christmas City Canoe Race, during the Christmas City Festival in 1977, my administrative assistant, Dan Fitzpatrick, and I challenged two administrators from Allentown. We came in second.

As mayor, I had a responsibility to test out the new tennis courts.

A number of lawsuits and problems delayed construction for over a year. Finally, the 800-car garage, which cost $4.3 million, was dedicated on December 10, 1976. About fifty City officials, businessmen and other dignitaries came out on a chilly morning for the official opening.

Unfortunately, even though the garage was completed, many of the buildings expected to provide business for it had not been built, or were being underutilized. The Plaza Mall never really did develop as hoped, and did not contribute much to the need for parking. Neither the convention center nor the performing arts theater were ever built. The downtown merchants instituted a "Park and Shop" program to encourage people to shop in the downtown area, with some success. Six months after it opened, revenues from the parking garage were showing steady increase. Still, the garage never earned as much as we projected while I was in office.

One of the organizations that the City of Bethlehem belonged to when I was mayor was the U.S. Conference of Mayors, as well as the Pennsylvania League of Cities and the National League of Cities. Some people wondered why we used these organizations, and what were the advantages for the City of Bethlehem. There was one very specific instance where the U.S. Conference of Mayors connection led to the passage of a piece of legislation that greatly benefitted the city.

The public works department was one of the areas where Bethlehem most needed help. None of the facilities at the time were very good, and there were multiple sites. The municipal buildings where we serviced the city's trucks, where the water department was located, and where other activities were housed all needed to be replaced. The ambulance center on Linden Street, for example, only had

Breaking ground for the new municipal garage are me, Charlie Brown and George Perhac.

Three mayors of Bethlehem *left to right,* Earl Schaffer, Gordon Payrow and Gordon Mowrer, celebrated the topping off of the Walnut Street parking garage.

room for two ambulances to park. The city had developed plans for a municipal garage at the end of Broad Street, near the Minsi Trail Bridge, but it did not have money to build such a facility.

The federal government was introducing a new program, an Economic Development Administration (EDA) grant, available to cities for one time only to help with public works activities. In May, 1977, a group of mayors traveled to Washington, D.C. to meet with the president of the United States. I went with this group specifically to tell him how much we needed this facility and how we needed money. President Jimmy Carter was very receptive to the idea; it was during a time of economic downturn, and he wanted to help.

At a U.S. Conference of Mayors meeting in July of 1976, I had met Governor Carter, then a candidate for president. I did a little interview with him for my radio program in Bethlehem, and we chatted for a while. He remembered Bethlehem, and during the interview he said,

> "I will never forget the hospitality and friendship and warm reception that I got in your area of Pennsylvania. . . . The results of the Pennsylvania primary were a major leap forward for my whole campaign. So I feel close to you and your listeners, and I'll never forget your early expression of support, Mr. Mayor, and the support I got in the primary from you."

When I asked about the programs that he would support as president that would help cities like Bethlehem, he mentioned a variety of areas, including transportation, law enforcement, and education. He especially mentioned that, in his opinion,

"We need to have maximum control of administration of these programs at the local levels of government, where the special needs and diversity of our communities can be recognized, and where local administrators who are responsible directly to the people on a day-to-day basis can monitor the effectiveness of the program as we go along."

When the grants were announced, Bethlehem was on the list to receive some money. I was personally invited to come to Washington, D.C. when Jimmy Carter signed the papers authorizing the program that would give Bethlehem this money. He signed the papers in the Rose Garden. It was an amazing experience for me: to be there in the White House Rose Garden with the president of the United States when he signed legislation that would give Bethlehem about $3 million.

After the signing ceremony, I was invited to meet with the president in the Oval Office. There I stood, in the office of the president of the United States, having a one-on-one chat with the president. I was even listed by name on the president's agenda that day. When I left the office, the official photographer took pictures. A few days later (this was in the days before instant photograph prints), the president signed the pictures and sent them to me with some notes. Needless to say, it was a fantastic experience.

When I left, I stood on the street corner looking back at the White House, and my heart started to beat about three times faster than normal. I remember thinking that someday, if I get to meet Jesus Christ in person, I wonder how fast my heart is going to beat then. That would be even more incredible than meeting the president of the United States. Somehow, I think Jimmy Carter would agree.

President Jimmy Carter signing the Public Works Jobs Bill in the Rose Garden. Behind on Carter's right is Senator Jennings Randolph of West Virginia, the chair of the Senate's Public Works Committee. On Carter's left is Abe Beame, mayor of New York City. Nobody knew who the guy in the striped suit immediately behind Carter was until a local reporter told them.

THE WHITE HOUSE			THE DAILY DIARY OF PRESIDENT JIMMY CARTER

LOCATION
THE WHITE HOUSE
WASHINGTON, D.C.

DATE (Mo., Day, Yr.)
MAY 13, 1977
TIME   DAY
6:00 a.m. FRIDAY

TIME		PHONE P=Placed R=Rec'd	ACTIVITY
From	To		
6:00		R	The President received a wake up call from the White House signal board operator.
6:25			The President went to his private office.
7:40	7:45		The President met with his Assistant for National Security Affairs, Zbigniew Brzezinski.
8:15	8:20		The President met with Mr. Brzezinski.
8:45	9:15		The President met with:
8:55	9:15		Frank B. Moore, Assistant for Congressional Liaison
			Hamilton Jordan, Assistant
9:30			The President went to the Rose Garden.
9:30	9:45		The President participated in a signing ceremony for H.R. 11, the Public Works Jobs Bill, and H.R. **4876**, the Economic Stimulus Appropriations Bill. For a list of attendees, see APPENDIX "A."
			Members of the press
9:30			The President addressed guests attending the ceremony.
9:45			The President returned to the Oval Office.
9:45	9:48		The President participated in a photo opportunity with Gordon B. Mowrer, Mayor, Bethlehem, Pennsylvania.
9:59		R	The President was telephoned by Mrs. Mark O. Hatfield, wife of the Senator (D-Oregon). The call was not completed.
10:00			The President went to the Cabinet Room.
10:00	11:02		The President met to discuss intelligence legislation with Members of the Senate Select Committee on Intelligence. For a list of attendees, see APPENDIX "B."
11:02			The President returned to his private office.
11:02			The President returned to the Rose Garden.

GPO : 1977 O-228-197

Page 1 of 4 Page(s).

One of my prized papers is a copy of President Jimmy Carter's daily diary, with my name on it.

The picture of the president signing the bill, watched by all the mayors and key legislators, with me front and center, was on the front page of every major newspaper in the United States the next day. The signing took place on Friday the 13th of May, 1977. It was a great day.

The following Tuesday was primary election day. I was running in the Democratic primary against Paul Marcincin, the City Council president, and Joseph Mangan, who had formerly worked for me as director of parks and public property. I thought I was going to do well, and even Marcincin's advisors expected me to win by a slim margin. Paul Marcincin *killed* me in the election; it wasn't even close. That election ended my political career as an elected official, other than coming back later for City Council. Within the space of five days, I had gone from a very high high to a very low low. The national newspaper coverage turned out not to help me at all, and may have done more harm than good.

Before I left office at the end of 1977, I got to help break ground to start the construction of the municipal services garage. It was planned to house the mechanical services, ambulance, streets department, water bureau and sewer maintenance, central warehouse, and all of the vehicles for those departments. The project was budgeted for $2 million. Much of that came from the federal grant, with the remainder of the federal money going for the Main Street project. The remaining $265,000 for the municipal building was allocated by City Council. The construction of this important building was accomplished with no debt for Bethlehem.

Even though I was not in office when it was completed, I was a part of getting the money that made it happen. That makes me feel good.

Chapter

10

Behind the Red Curtains: The Open Door Policy

During all of my years in office, one of my basic philosophical beliefs was that government should be responsive, as well as responsible, to its citizens. That meant that government should also be open and accessible to them. One of the first things I discovered when I came in as mayor was that it was very difficult for an ordinary citizen to get through to various City Hall offices and departments. Members of the public would call, and they would get the runaround: it would be somebody else's responsibility, and they would have to go to two or three places and still the complaint would not always be handled.

I thought we needed to have somebody in the mayor's office who could help people when they called with a problem. So we hired Pat Kesling, and we made her an ombudsman, responsible for dealing with citizens' complaints. If anybody had a problem, they would call City Hall and she would take care of them and handle the complaint through to completion. She would make the contact with the proper department head or the person responsible for getting the job done. If they did not listen to her, she would say something to me and I would get on them. By the second year of my administration, we

During a South Side walking tour in July, 1976, Mrs. Nellie Rodrigues and Mrs. Helen Roma talked with me, Jay Howard, Len Righi, and Pat Ruggiero, as Bill Grubb and Pat Kesling looked on. *Courtesy the Express-Times*

publicized a special telephone number for people to call for city-related complaints, problems or information. We called it the Service and Information Office, part of the mayor's office. It was a way of communicating with the people, letting them know that we were there, and that we cared.

We also tried a variety of ways to let people know what the city government was doing. We arranged for the local public television station, WLVT Channel 39, and local cable television stations to carry some programs about what Bethlehem government was doing. I visited a variety of citizen groups to present a slide show depicting what had happened in Bethlehem in the last few years.

We tried to keep the press informed of what was going on. We published an annual insert in the *Bethlehem Globe-Times* for several years, with a report of what the city had done in the past year. These were all ways of communicating directly with the public. My administration improved communications tremendously.

I began a daily radio program on WGPA at 12:10 p.m., talking about local topics and interviewing some special visitors to the community. Sometimes during the program I walked around the city with a tape recorder, greeting people and asking them why they came to Bethlehem and what they thought of Bethlehem. I had some wonderful experiences. One lady who was visiting said that she was so happy to be here with the Morivians (or maybe she said "Morahvians," I remember that she mispronounced the word). She wanted to know if there were any of them alive today. I assured her that there were. Talking to another woman on the West Side led me to conclude, on the air, that, "Frankly on the walking tours, we've found out that a lot of people, the vast majority, are really very satisfied, and I hope you are, too."

Making government accessible to every citizen was what we had in mind when we established what we called "Open Door" on Wednesday afternoons. Every Wednesday afternoon after my noon-time Rotary meeting, I would go back to City Hall. For the rest of that afternoon, anyone who wanted to come in to see the mayor could do so, without an appointment, with any issue or opinion that he or she had in mind. The mayor would listen to the problem and, if necessary, would call in the appropriate department head, to make sure that things were processed. All the department heads were required to be at City Hall on Wednesday afternoon, and when there was an issue that was related to their department, they would be called to come to the mayor's office. That meant that they were available on short notice, but they would not have to sit around and wait until people would come in (or not come in). If it was a police problem, for example, we would call the police commissioner to come in. This program showed that we cared, that we were willing to listen, and that City Hall was accessible to citizens, even without an appointment.

This was a new feature. In some ways it was similar to the "courtesy of the floor" that City Council has now, where anyone can come to a Council meeting and speak about any subject they want. The press particularly enjoyed this program, as they were also free to come in when there were problems that they wanted to discuss.

My staff shared in this effort as well. Joan Schrei, who was my secretary at the time, learned that when people called, we responded to them because we cared about them. Joan was often the one who lined up the visitors and got them ready to come into my office. Pat Kesling usually joined me during these sessions, so that she could facilitate any solutions.

During the years that we had Open Door, there was never a Wednesday that no one came. At least one person came on every Wednesday, and one afternoon there were thirty-seven people who came to see me. There was a tremendous variety of things that people would come in to ask about and talk about. It turned out to be a wonderful experience for me, as I got to meet a lot of people that I had not met before. Some of the conversations which began on a Wednesday afternoon had further-reaching consequences than any of us could have imagined.

Debbie Merkle and her teacher, David Drabic, came to ask for help so that she could visit her pen pal in Japan. We discussed Japanese culture, like the bonsai tree I am holding.

One of the very interesting folks who came in to Open Door one Wednesday afternoon in 1977 was a teacher by the name of David Drabic. David was teaching sixth grade at Marvine School. He had a student, Debbie Merkle, who was from the Marvine area. When she was in Drabic's class, she had established a pen pal relationship with a student from Japan. Now, several years later, she wanted to go visit this pen pal. They decided that she would try to raise some money, and that they would come in and see the mayor, and see if he could help. She was doing babysitting to raise money, and any other kind of job that a fifteen-year-old girl could get. I was very impressed with her. We decided at City Hall to try to help her, and we did. She continued writing to her pen pal friend, Dave Drabic helped her raise some money, and I think the help from City Hall made the difference. She did get to go to Japan.

Interestingly enough, after she came back her pen pal, Yumi Takahashi, decided she wanted to come over here and visit. They made arrangements for a swap visit, and the girl came and visited Bethlehem two years later. Neither woman has been back to visit the other since then, but they do remain in touch and write several times a year.

One Wednesday afternoon, a psychic came in to see me. She sat down and said to me, "Let me feel your wedding ring." I gave her my wedding ring, and she hemmed and hawed around it, and she finally said, "You've been planning a trip." That morning, I had thrown away a flyer that had come from the Allentown Sister City program, advertising a trip to their Sister City, Tiberias, in Israel. The trip was to the Holy Land, a place that I had always wanted to see someday. I thought, "There's no way she could have known that I was planning a trip." The only person I had talked to about the trip was my wife, and we had decided we could not afford it. Besides, it was Allentown's Sister City, and they probably would not want someone from Bethlehem going with them. The psychic said to me, "You've been thinking about going, but this morning you decided not to go." I said, "That is correct, I can't believe you knew that." She said, "I want to encourage you to reexamine it and go, because it will be a wonderful experience for you."

I went home that day and called Phil Berman, who was then the president of Hess's and very involved in the Allentown Sister City program. I asked how he would feel about the mayor of Bethlehem going to the Holy Land and Tiberias with the Sister City trip. He said they would love to have me, and if I went and paid my way, they would let my wife go for half price. Well, I thought, when will I ever get an opportunity like this again? So I went home and I said to Mary, "You know, if you decide to go, you'll go for half price. I don't see how we can say no." She decided she would love to go.

So in November, 1977, we went on the Sister City Tiberias trip with the Allentown people. We met with the mayor of Jerusalem, Teddy Kollek, and we had lunch and dinner with the mayor of Tiberias. We also visited with the mayor of Bethlehem (the one in Israel), both in his home and in his gift shop business. We traveled around to all the usual places and got in to special locations. When we went to the birthplace of Jesus, we went down into an area where they claim he slept in his swaddling clothes. Normally it is a very quiet, reverent place. Because we were from Bethlehem (the other one), we got to sing "O Little Town of Bethlehem" when we were there. Our guides said it was very unusual to have someone sing in that place. It was a unique and wonderful trip, and it all happened because of Open Door.

One of the areas that came up many times in Open Door was when people had a problem with something that was going on in the city. For example, someone was putting in a group home, and some of the neighbors around the area did not particularly want it. This happened frequently when there were group homes, or homes for ex-prisoners, or homes for people with special needs or emotional problems. With Open Door, people at least had a place to come and air their thoughts, and we always took them seriously. We would visit the location and make sure it was not within a school zone, for example. But these kinds of facilities are very difficult to place, and neighbors are usually not very happy.

I remember one incident in particular, which I think had to do with Valley Youth House. A lady lived next door to where some kids were going to be staying, and she initially was very, very upset about it. She talked to the people who were involved, and when she learned what was going on, she decided that when these kids moved in, she was going to make them an apple pie. So she baked an apple pie, and took it over to the kids. From that day forward, she was "Grandma." And when wintertime came and the snow needed shoveling, and in the summer when the grass needed cutting, these kids cut her grass, shoveled her snow, and cleaned off her porch. She became the best friends with them. It was nice to see that some people could respond positively after they learned about these activities.

There were a lot of neighborhood squabbles, with people complaining about what their neighbors did. Somebody had junk piled up in the backyard next door; a resident would come in and tell us about it. We would get the health department to check it, and make sure it was not a hazard. If a house was left to deteriorate and was not cared for, we would have our housing authority check that. If there were health hazards in somebody's back yard, we would have the health people come and check. We were able to follow up on a lot of complaints.

We quickly learned that Wednesday afternoon was often used to air complaints. During the leaf season when leaves were not picked up at certain areas, people would come in to complain about it. We would get somebody out to clean the leaves up; we responded to their complaints. From time to time there would be someone who would come in to talk about vandalism in the parks, or what was going on at night in the parks, encouraging us to send police around to check and recheck to make sure that all was well. We would be attentive to all kinds of issues. We were there to listen to what people had to say, and then to try to do something about their problem, to let them know they were important. When people had an issue, they could come right to the mayor, and he would call his key people, and they would respond.

Every once in a while there would be a major problem, like a non-functioning storm sewer. Sometimes we would have a group of twenty or thirty people whose storm sewers had backed up, all coming in on Wednesday afternoon. So we would get the appropriate people from the water authority to go check it out and to follow up on it and make sure the problem was corrected. I know that there were serious problems on Buckingham Drive in north Bethlehem; the sewer had backed up, and the storm sewer had backed up, and it badly needed attention. We were able to get that resolved.

There was an industry called Waylite that had taken over one of Bethlehem Steel's facilities. Their process to reuse slag, a waste product from steel-making, and turn it into an ingredient for construction materials produced very loud, banging noises, sometimes at two and three o'clock in the morning. The noise was unbelievable, especially coming across the river. A group of neighbors from Church Street came to complain one Wednesday afternoon. Susan Parks remembers coming with the neighbors, sitting in a circle and talking about the noise problem. City employees got decibel equipment to measure the noise, which certainly exceeded allowable levels at the time. We met with the company, and tried to get them to start new methods so that they would not make so much loud noise. City Council tried to encourage them to change, and fined them on numerous occasions. It took a while, but eventually the industry was sold, and the noise finally stopped.

Sometimes, there was not much that we could do,

Sampson Taylor and his wife, Lillian, came to see me at Open Door from time to time. Taylor was a steelworker, very active in the union, and a really good person.

The painting on the wall behind me *(see close-up below)* shows the Hill-to-Hill Bridge back in the 1940s, and possibly early '50s, with Christmas decorations. People used to line up there to see Bethlehem at Christmas time. The painting is absolutely magnificent.

even though we tried. Someone came in to complain about the adult bookstore at the Five Points on the South Side. As a result of that Wednesday afternoon visit, the police commissioner, Bob Galle, and I went to check it out. Unfortunately, we couldn't do a whole lot about it at the time. Toby Clauser used to come in quite frequently concerning serious problems with speeding on Wyandotte Street hill, particularly with trucks. We really tried to help (there is more about this in the police chapter), but I think those problems still continue today.

We had people who wanted to have their pictures taken sitting in the mayor's chair, so Wednesday afternoon was the time that people had the right to come in and sit in the mayor's chair, or have their children sit in the mayor's chair, and take a picture. Sometimes they wanted to meet the mayor, and this was an opportunity to meet the mayor. This was important for a lot of people.

Sometimes there were classes in schools that wanted to tour the mayor's office and show their students the mayor's office. Often we would allow that to happen on Wednesday afternoon. The class could come through and they could see a little bit about what goes on at City Hall and ask the mayor questions, or maybe talk to specific department heads.

Sometimes people came who were interested in a job. We would introduce them to the process of getting an interview so they could apply and they would know what jobs were available.

Some strange things happened during Open Door as well. One afternoon about 4:15, a lady who was dressed rather provocatively came in and said she wanted to talk to the mayor. The office normally closed at 4:30, so most people were getting ready to leave for the day. Pat Kesling had asked to go home a little early, because there was an evening event she had to attend. But when she saw this lady coming in to see me, she decided to stay.

This lady was kind of out of touch with reality, and I suspect she had some emotional problems. She said she was seeing Frank Sinatra and Tony Bennett and some people connected with the Mafia, and she was afraid that they were going to come and get her some night. She wanted police protection. During the interview we found out that she lived in Hellertown, and therefore was not in our jurisdiction. We said that we were sorry, but we could not help her because Bethlehem police do not cover Hellertown.

On one of the Wednesday afternoons, word had somehow come to the mayor's office that there was somebody coming in to kill me. The police were notified. We had two plainclothes officers in the back entrance to my office where they could keep watch on what would be going on. We had plainclothesmen out in the lobby where the elevator lets out, so that they could eye everybody who would come. Supposedly the person who was coming to do it did not have a gun, and was there because of something to do with Little League. Joan was very nervous as she waited for this person to arrive. Fortunately, nothing actually happened.

If someone had wanted to hurt the mayor, we inadvertently made it easy to tell where the mayor's office was, even from outside of City Hall. When I took office, the twelve-year-old draperies in my office and my secretary's office next door were very worn. We ordered new drapes for the mayor's office. After consultation with several staff members, we selected a colorful red and orange striped fabric accented with black thread. They gave the office a warm, inviting feel. My secretary, Joan, whose office had draperies of the same fabric, even commented that when the afternoon sun shone through them, the beige walls turned pink. People who came for Open Door frequently remarked appreciatively on how inviting the office appeared.

From the exterior of the building, the red curtains were very visible compared to the rest of the windows with neutral draperies. One man complained that they made the windows on the second floor at the southwest corner look "like a bawdy house."[1] He stopped in one day to register a complaint, but I was in Houston for a National League of Cities conference. That was one of the few complaints we received that we ignored.

Open Door was not only about complaints and problems. Once in a while people brought in some very creative ideas and suggestions. For example, Hans Wuerth, a professor of German at Moravian College, came in to see us about making bicycle paths in Bethlehem. We thought that was a timely suggestion, and worked to make it happen.

I remember handicapped people coming in, particularly around the times when there were activities going on in the city, complaining that the curbs and gutters made the sidewalks inaccessible for handicapped people, and there were no parking facilities for them. It is difficult to imagine now, because today that has changed dramatically. But when I was mayor back in the '70s, we did not have sidewalks that were made easy for wheelchairs, and there were no parking spaces for people with handicaps.

---

[1]"Eye for symmetry sees a red flag in mayor's drapes," Anne Kovalenko, *Morning Call*, December 5, 1974, p. 54.

Paul Reitmeir was one who used to come into my office concerning handicapped people and accessibility; he served on the Housing Authority, and has been a fine citizen of Bethlehem. He was in a wheelchair himself, and could give me knowledgeable advice. As a result of those conversations, we started the process of putting in sloping curb ramps so that people with handicaps (or baby strollers) could get up and down sidewalks easily. We also created reserved parking for handicapped people in special zones. We did not have those things before I came in; they are two improvements that came out of Open Door. People were very appreciative of our efforts.

In June of 1974, a couple had recently moved to Bethlehem. They read in the newspaper that the mayor was available on Wednesday afternoon, and they thought they would stop by, introduce themselves as new residents, and learn more about what goes on in Bethlehem. So one Wednesday afternoon, Lester and Suzy Titlow came to the mayor's office. We had a nice discussion. Today Lester and Suzy Titlow live in Moravian Village, just down the street from where my wife and I live. After all these years, they still remember the impact of that initial friendly "Hello" on a Wednesday afternoon.

The overall goal of Open Door was to open communications so people would feel that the mayor's office was accessible and the people in the mayor's office cared about them. I think we accomplished this.

Chapter

11

The Comeback Kid

Nine years after I left City Hall at the conclusion of my term as mayor, in early January, 1987, my wife and I were taking a mid-winter vacation in Jamaica. I was given a message to telephone Paul Calvo, a member of City Council. My first response was, "Uh oh, I know what this is all about." I phoned him, and he asked if I would consider coming back and being mayor of Bethlehem for one year. I told him that if they really wanted me I would give it serious consideration.

The next thing I knew, Jack Lawrence, the president of City Council, called to ask how soon I could come home. I said, "Hey, I hear that it's snowing in Bethlehem, and there is no way I'm going to rush to get home." We came home at the end of our scheduled vacation. Then I had a third phone call, asking which judge I wanted to use for the installation! Within two weeks, Paul Marcincin had been removed as mayor and I was selected, appointed and sworn in as the new mayor.

To many political observers, my selection to succeed Marcincin represented the "ultimate irony," as the *Globe-Times* put it.[1] In October, 1973, as I was running for

---

[1] "Many see irony in Mowrer's return," Sandy McClure, *Bethlehem Globe-Times*, January 26, 1987, p. 1.

When people came to my office to talk, I usually sat in a rocking chair.

mayor, Bethlehem passed an ordinance limiting the mayor to two consecutive terms in office. The ordinance was pushed by Paul Marcincin, then president of City Council, and it was widely believed that its purpose was to limit my future ability to continue in office. I was elected as mayor the next month, at the time the youngest mayor ever to be elected in Bethlehem.

In May of 1977, Paul Marcincin beat me in the primary election as I was running for my second term as mayor. He was elected as mayor, served his term of four years, and was elected to a second term. At the end of his second term, the city's legal bureau ruled that the 1973 ordinance was invalid. Marcincin ran for a third term and was elected. City Council brought suit, claiming that the law limiting a mayor to two consecutive terms was indeed valid and that Marcincin had been elected to a third term illegally. Marcincin served for one year before the Pennsylvania Supreme Court agreed with City Council that the ordinance limiting him to two terms was valid. The court declared that he was no longer mayor on January 13, 1987.

Jack Downing, the city's business manager, was appointed mayor until a new one could be selected, and he and Paul Calvo both turned down the opportunity to become mayor. On Monday, January 19, Paul Calvo called me in Jamaica. By Sunday, January 25, the newspaper listed the names of five possible candidates to be mayor. I was named as mayor the next day, and was sworn in on Tuesday, January 27. The same ordinance that was passed to keep me out was the one that brought me back.

After nine years, I was back in the mayor's office in City Hall, but only for one year. In announcing my appointment, Jack Lawrence noted that, "Mr. Mowrer, as a former mayor of the City of Bethlehem, is a well-qualified individual who is most capable of fulfilling the duties of the office during this interim period. Gordon Mowrer is an admirable and learned individual who has the respect of the community."[2] I was selected because of my previous experience as mayor, and also because I did not intend to seek election as mayor at the end of the year. A one-year appointment would give some stability to the office, and allowed time to hold an election for the next mayor without rushing. There would be no incumbent to benefit from that designation in the coming election. The Morning Call ran an editorial that declared, "Gordon Mowrer's return to City Hall is a welcome relief."[3]

My priorities for this year were to:
- ✓ focus on obtaining new jobs for the area to replace those being lost at Bethlehem Steel and Mack Trucks
- ✓ emphasize solid waste issues

[2]Quoted in "Mowrer will become Bethlehem Mayor," Sandy McClure, Bethlehem Globe-Times, January 26, 1987, p. 1.

[3]"Welcome back, Mayor Mowrer," Morning Call, January 28, 1987, p. A12.

✓   re-institute the Open Door program, which my predecessor had closed

In my first term as mayor, the city's history had inspired me to redirect the development of downtown Bethlehem to preserve and build on this heritage. In this term, I again turned to the city's history and heritage to inspire a plan of economic development, promoting year-round tourism in the area. Much of my year in office was spent on this effort. In May I hired Eric Herrenkohl as a student intern to research tourism and how cities similar to Bethlehem were promoting it. By July, a tourism questionnaire was printed in the newspaper, to solicit the public's view of how tourism funding should be spent, what organization should be responsible, and whether more tourism events should be created. By September I had completed a *Tourism Proposal for the City of Bethlehem.* We made the proposal into a video, and I spent the remainder of the year presenting the idea to community groups and the public. The proposal was endorsed by the Bethlehem Chamber of Commerce. The entire proposal is reprinted as an appendix to this book.

Solid waste issues also took quite a bit of my time. We dealt with problems with Waylite, a company located on the South Side across the Lehigh River from Nisky Hill Cemetery, for much of the year. The company processed slag, a waste product from steel-making, into a powder used in construction materials. Unfortunately, the process created both a rotten egg-like odor and explosion-like noises at all hours of the day and night. Residents came to complain about it at Open Door. Even though City Council tried to work with them to solve both issues, the company was repeatedly fined. Toward the end of my year in office, the company closed that plant.

Speaking at the dedication of the new landfill *left,* and the place mat for the dedication breakfast at the new landfill

Other solid waste issues we dealt with during the year were a proposed regional solid waste incinerator in Bethlehem, problems with Bethlehem's landfill, the possibility of a new sewage treatment plant in Salisbury Township at the western end of Bethlehem, closing the mulch pile on Schoenersville Road and dealing with other garbage and recycling issues.

Solid waste does not usually provide many good stories, but there was one event that took place during this year that was a little unusual. To celebrate the opening of the expanded landfill, a project that had taken seven years to complete, we decided to invite about thirty officials to breakfast – at the landfill. Under a red and white canopy, we served coffee, fast food breakfast sandwiches, pastries and speeches, as garbage trucks came and went nearby conducting landfill business as usual. The place settings included a special place mat cut from the same material as the plastic liner that was installed to prevent groundwater contamination, as well as candlesticks and vases of roses. Carol Thompson, a local harpist, provided music. It was a memorable event.

One area which occupied quite a bit of my time during that year was AIDS. The disease had only been identified a few years before that, and the public knew little about it except that it seemed to be very contagious and always fatal. I had first-hand knowledge of the disease and its effects because I was an associate chaplain at St. Luke's Hospital, where I visited and counseled with AIDS patients and their families. I also knew that many of the "facts" of the disease and its transmission were misunderstood.

People were so fearful of contracting the disease that one day, after two women who had accompanied a suspect with AIDS had used the bathroom in the police station, the police closed the bathroom. No one was willing to clean it. To show that this was unacceptable and that there was no risk of contracting AIDS through a public toilet, I called the City Health Director, Glen Cooper, and the city's Health Bureau Medical Director, Dr. John M. Snyder. The three of us went down and cleaned the ladies' room ourselves. We got our picture in the newspaper, scrubbing away.

In April at a joint press conference, Mayor Joseph Daddona of Allentown, Mayor Sal Panto of Easton, and I announced that the three cities were developing a joint policy on how to handle persons with AIDS, especially in the areas of prevention and protection. Later in the year, Lt. Governor Mark Singel visited the Lehigh Valley to ask what local leaders considered to be major concerns. I asked him if the state could help provide local educators on the topic of AIDS. In August, the three mayors of Bethlehem, Allentown and Easton combined in a joint AIDS effort to provide education, hiring, and a full-time educator. That meant, for Bethlehem, that the City would distribute condoms at clinics, promote AIDS education to its City employees, and hire an AIDS educator as part of the City staff. On December 9, an article was published in the *Bethlehem Globe-Times*, in which I called AIDS "the most critical issue of the very near future."[4]

In February, 1988, Jose Cruz was hired by the City of Bethlehem as its first AIDS counselor.

Another *Globe-Times* article published at the end of the year, which summarized editorials from 1987, noted that my "most notable impact is his commitment . . . to an activist role in areas of public health."[5] Besides AIDS, I also instituted a policy requiring City employees to wear seatbelts while on City business, whether they drove a City vehicle or their own. As an insurance agent, I had seen many times that seatbelts saved lives if the vehicle was involved in an accident.

Another public health issue which showed that Bethlehem was ahead of its time was smoking in City Hall. During my tenure the Smoking Committee implemented phase one of a ban on smoking in the building, with the exception of a few indoor areas. Phase two included banning smoking at City Hall entirely, as well as in other City-owned buildings such as fire stations and the municipal garage. Two decades after Bethlehem's efforts, smoking in all public buildings in Pennsylvania was banned.

_____

[4]"Time to do something about AIDS is now, Mayor Mowrer says," Pat Kesling, p. D4.

[5]"The issues of '87," December 31, 1987, p. A6.

Looking back after more than twenty years, it is difficult to imagine that in 1987, the Bethlehem City offices generally were not computerized. Even though I had established a computer council in my first year as mayor in 1974, there was still much more to do. I was quoted as saying that the offices were "in the Dark Ages," technologically speaking, and I tried to make computerizing the City operations one of my priorities. It took all year, but I was able to hire a consulting firm to get the offices computerized, and I made sure that money for it was included in the 1988 budget.

During 1987, I decided that I needed a college intern to help in the mayor's office. We hired Eric Herrenkohl, a student from Bethlehem who was attending the University of Michigan, and gave him the special assignment to research tourism. Over twenty years later, he is now the founder and president of Herrenkohl Consulting, a recruiting and training company in the Philadelphia area. Eric remembers some of the highlights of his time in my office:

- that I was willing to delegate significant responsibilities. He remembers that as a nineteen-year-old, he helped to choose Bethlehem's next police commissioner.
- that I surrounded myself with good people, especially my administrative assistant, Barbara Caldwell, and others
- that I brought tremendous energy to the job, was always positive, held my staff to high standards, and taught him to be proactive

One area of the mayor's job that took a great deal of time, but which people usually think very little about, was the ceremonial aspect of the job. During this one year, I performed several weddings, which I had also done during

Auctioning the opportunity to be "Mayor for a Day" at a WLVT-TV auction are the three Lehigh Valley mayors: Joe Daddona, Allentown; Gordon Mowrer, Bethlehem; and Sal Panto, Easton. We were such a serious bunch!

my first term in office. In fact, I performed two weddings on my final day in office. I issued proclamations for Afghanistan Day, Portuguese Heritage Day and Bastille

Day. I entertained visitors from several cities in Germany that wished to become Sister Cities with Bethlehem, including a delegation from Schwäbisch Gmünd. I proclaimed Better Hearing and Speech Month and National Hospital Week. I attended meetings of the Women's Club (yes, really!), the Christian Business Men's committee, the Musikfest International Ball and St. Luke's Benefit Ball, and the Windish Society's 75th anniversary dinner. I hosted the annual Advent Breakfast, and gave everyone who attended a kiss (the chocolate kind, from the centerpieces). I joined with Mayor Daddona of Allentown and Mayor Panto of Easton at a Channel 39 benefit event to auction off the opportunity to be "Mayor for a Day." At the "Run for the Roses" in Lancaster, I competed with three other mayors, in addition to a lot of other runners. I was not the first mayor to cross the finish line, but I am very proud that I finished before Mayor Daddona!

For some reason, what I wore to various functions was of interest to newspaper reporters, if not their readers. I was one of the models in the Voluntary Action Center fashion show. At the opening of the Christmas City Fair, the newspaper commented on my yellow shirt and light green plaid slacks. At the Mayor's Cup soccer match, I was dressed (I thought appropriately) in jogging shorts and a sleeveless shirt. I wore black tie to the Musikfest Ball and other similar events. At the police raid where I was given (and did not wear) a bulletproof vest with a hole in it, the newspaper mentioned that I dressed down, wearing blue jeans with paint on them, a scruffy sweater, running shoes and a Grateful Dead cap.

At the end of my term, I presented a list of *Future Issues to be Addressed for the City of Bethlehem* to the members of City Council and mayor-elect Ken Smith.

Under management-related needs, I included improving the use of technology at City Hall, especially implementing the use of computers and upgrading the antiquated telephone communication system; providing management training and development programs for staff; reexamining policies on sick leave and injuries as well as the pay scale for the mayor; and building training facilities for the police and fire departments. Under program development needs, I included developing a Bethlehem Tourism Authority, rethinking the policy of using city maintenance personnel to help non-profit organizations, and refurbishing the ice house on Sand Island for some use to be determined. In all I suggested twenty-one issues which needed serious consideration in the future.

Looking back over my one-year term, I think that for me, politics was better the second time around. It is good that I was in office for only one year. I was able to accomplish some goals without the need to run for re-election. I was able to cooperate better with the members of City Council this time, without worrying about running against some of them in the future. Since my first term in office, I had learned to listen more to department heads. But while I accomplished some things and laid the foundation for other projects, I was frustrated that government still moved more slowly than I wanted. Some things just do not change.

February 15, 1988 was proclaimed "Gordon B. Mowrer Day" in Bethlehem, Allentown and Easton by the three mayors, and I was honored with a reception at the Hotel Bethlehem attended by about 200 friends. Northampton County Judge William F. Moran said that I had "turned a year of crisis into a year of achievement."

Chapter

12

Family Views

A career in politics almost always involves not only the politician, but also the family of the politician. Even when the politician tries to keep the family out of the spotlight, it is very difficult to accomplish, as many present-day news stories demonstrate.

Occasionally the family can share in a special event away from the limelight. One year when I was mayor the real Santa Claus came to Bethlehem. He was a real person who had changed his name to Santa C. Claus. He looked very much like Santa Claus, and would come and meet with people. Kids would come from everywhere to see him. We had him over to our house to dinner one night. I told the kids we were having a surprise visitor. I put a present for each child on the front porch, so when Mr. Claus arrived, he picked them up and brought the presents in to give to each of our three kids. We had the most marvelous supper you could possibly imagine.

My wife and children were always involved in my political career, sometimes unwillingly, sometimes unwittingly. It is only fair that I give them a chance to tell some of their own stories.

My family was at my side when I was installed as mayor in 1974. The oath of office was administered by Judge Al Williams. *Courtesy the Morning Call*

The mayor's family outside our house in 1977

Mary's Perspective

When Gordie asked me to write how I felt about his years as mayor, I balked. I am not a "front stage" person; I do not like to be in the spotlight. But I do have some thoughts and stories which he has persuaded me to share.

During those political years, not only Gordy[1] and I, but also our whole family was subject to review by our constituency. At least, that's what I thought.

When Gordy was first elected, our children were quite young, in elementary school, in fact. And Meg was a very young child, not even in preschool. She intensely disliked going to the grocery store, and periodically she objected strenuously, very loudly. I pictured people whispering about that screaming Mowrer child. To this day I am very sympathetic when I hear or see some mother in a similar situation.

I can remember the first night Gordy arrived home from City Hall. The garage led directly into the kitchen, where the usual pre-dinner chaos was going on. He came in and stood at the door and announced he was home and started barking out orders! I remember turning around and saying, "This is your home and family, not City Hall." He burst out laughing and agreed. This leads me to a major point I want to make. Political families are human and fallible, and "stuff" often happens.

We went to a lot of political functions and I often had to sit with Gordy at the head table. I was quite pregnant with Meg when Gordy was on City Council the first time. At one political dinner, as the head table was being introduced I

---

[1]It is not a typo that Mary sometimes spells my name Gordie and sometimes Gordy. I spell it both ways myself.

Mary and Meg　*Courtesy the Morning Call*

realized that my maternity dress was identical to the one worn by the Democratic chairwoman sitting at the other end of the head table. The master of ceremonies did not miss this duplication, and made a big deal of it.

At a luncheon later in the campaign, I was seated at one end of the head table. I was the only woman at the head table, and most of the others, except for Gordie, were priests. I think it was a jubilee celebration. The table was set on a platform. Unfortunately, we did not realize how narrow the platform was. When we were seated after the opening grace, my chair toppled backwards, and I with it. Imagine my embarrassment when several clergymen jumped down and picked me up!

Because our social lives revolved mainly around political affairs, I really missed my own friends with whom I had spent most of our early years of marriage. I had to drop out of bridge clubs and lunch groups and volunteer activities. On the rare occasions when I did see my friends, they would ask what I talked about at political affairs, and what "these people" did, as if they were different. They eventually discovered, as did we, that political and non-political people are very much alike, having a deep love of friends, family, and fun. Many "political" folks became our close friends as we all discovered that people are people, no matter what you do or whom you support politically.

Finally, I learned one very important lesson. I experienced first-hand living as a family member of someone involved in politics. Before Gordy became mayor, I figured most "politicians" were folks of questionable character, and I wondered what kinds of families they might have. Did they even have families? I learned by experience that many "politicians" are deeply committed people who want only the best for their constituency. During their time in office, they and their families will often be criticized, no matter what they do.

After experiencing life in a political family first-hand, I now admire those involved in public life. Most of them mean well and try to do their best. They should not be criticized. They should be aided in any way possible.

I had a couple of interesting experiences while Gordy was mayor, things that never happened to me before or after he was mayor. In all of my driving experience, which wasn't *that* much, I never got any tickets until my husband became mayor. One day I went to what was then First Valley Bank (now Bank of America), the branch on Linden Street, to cash a check so I could go grocery shopping. Of

Happy Birthday, Bethlehem! You see Anne McGeady underneath the arm of Mary Mowrer, who is cutting the top of the cake, and Meg Mowrer observing from below. It was a wonderful celebration on July 16,1977, the 60th anniversary of the incorporation of Bethlehem. *Courtesy the Morning Call*

course, I had to take all three children with me. Without thinking, I just pulled up beside the bank and went inside.

The way that bank was laid out, you could be writing the slip to withdraw funds and look out the window to see where your car was parked. One of the children said, "Hey, look, Mom, the police are doing something to your car." I looked up, and there he was, writing a ticket. I went running out, and the three children went running after me, and I said, "No, no, no, no! What are you doing?" He said, "I'm giving you a ticket for parking the wrong way on this side of the street." He wasn't going to take it back, so I just said, "OK, give me the ticket."

I got the children together and said, "Let's get into the car; we're going to go pay this ticket right away, before it gets old." We bundled into the car, and I drove down to City Hall. I was really a little annoyed because I didn't know you couldn't park that way. The children were all really excited – "Mommy got a ticket!" I went in to the police sergeant, to the desk where you are supposed to pay the fine. The sergeant said, "Oh, you got a parking ticket, parking the wrong way on the street." I said in a disgusted tone, "Yeah!" He asked, "You're not going to pay it, are you?" and I said, "Of course I'm going to pay it, I did something wrong." He said, "Ummm, the families don't usually pay." I said, "This one does."

I dug in my pocketbook to get out whatever the fine was, and of course, since I was on my way to the bank to get cash, I had no money. It wasn't bad enough that I got a ticket, and then had to appear with three children who were saying "My Mom got a ticket!" and making lots of noise. The sergeant said, "Mrs. Mowrer, why don't you just go upstairs and talk to your husband?" We went upstairs, and I told Gordy about my ticket. He gave me the money to pay the fine, and I went back down and I paid it. So now I am very careful about how I park on the street, on what side of the street. That was the first ticket I got.

The second one was a number of years later. It was a hot Saturday afternoon in June, the day before Father's Day. Meg was just a little girl, about three or four years old, and she and I had gone to buy an ice cream cake for her father. I was hurrying because I wanted to get the cake home before it melted. We were zipping along Macada Road, and next thing I knew, there was a police car motioning for me to pull over to the side of the road. I noticed along Macada Road there were a number of cars that had been pulled over. They pulled us over onto Artemis Drive, which went off of Macada Road, and told me I had been speeding. As I looked around I saw a number of my neighbors; we had all been caught in this speed trap. I sat there and he wrote this ticket for me while my cake melted – I can remember it dripping all over and Meg "cleaning up" the drips with her fingers and really enjoying the whole thing. Of course, that counted points against my driving record. I was very, very upset about it, and made up my mind that I was not going to get any more tickets, at least not when my husband was mayor. And I didn't.

But my sister-in-law, Barbara Mowrer, took advantage of the name when she went down to the country club to play tennis. She was on the South Side, and there's a stop sign where you turn right to go onto Packer. She did not always stop for it. One time when she slid through, the police stopped her and asked for her driver's license. When she gave them her license, they looked at it and saw the name Mowrer, and an officer said, "Oh, Mrs. Mowrer, I'm sorry, I didn't realize it was you. That's OK." And they let her go! I know that the police thought it was me, and I had nothing to do with it.

On one other occasion I was driving on New Street, on my way home, and I went through a yellow caution light. I was not going very fast, and I probably could have stopped, but I didn't. Meg was in the car seat in the back seat of the car, and she was pretty little, probably a year old or thereabouts. This policeman pulled me over, and told me that I had gone through a caution light. He said, "Oh, Mrs. Mowrer, here you have that lovely little girl in the back seat, and you know you could have caused an accident. I know it was a caution light, but you're not supposed to go through caution lights. I'm going to let you go this time, but I want you to always remember this so you never do it again." I think he enjoyed lecturing me.

I am not going to tell you I never go through caution lights, but I have never gone through any that I did not remember the lecture I got from that policeman.

George's Perspective

What would a book of memories of the political years of Gordon Mowrer be without some perspective from his family, who walked side-by-side with him much of the time? Although that was over thirty years ago, and I was only ten or so years old, I still have some pretty profound memories.

As I gathered my thoughts about those years and began writing them down, I found that overall, my time as the "Mayor's Son" was really good.

The Good Stuff

The Trips

If someone were to ask me what the best part of being the mayor's son was, right off the top of my head, in an

Three generations of Mowrer men: my father, my son George, myself and my brother Tip

instant, I would say "the trips." Over those four years (1973-1977) I had the opportunity to travel to California, Arizona, Florida, Puerto Rico, Boston, and of course, Japan and Hawaii.

On these trips, I had the opportunity to do and experience things I probably would never have done, if my dad were not the mayor. He was a busy guy and out most evenings at one event or the other. We didn't spend a lot of time with him. So when these trips came along, he looked at them as opportunities for some quality time with his family. Sure, there were all the meetings, but there was the time before or after the meetings, or before or after the conference, when he would hang out with his family.

The Mayors' Conferences

I loved these conferences. They were usually held in places where families would want to go. And interestingly, many of the mayors brought their families and kids along. And like other conference types of things, there were special programs set up for spouses and children. And of course, my sister Ruthie and I loved these things. There we were, hanging out with mayors' kids from all over the country. I couldn't wrap my arms around it then, but as I look back now, thirty-plus years later, it was pretty astounding to have a hundred mayor's kids do day trips to the likes of amusement parks, national parks, and other cool entertainment destinations.

Over the years many of the same kids returned, so some relationships began to develop. The mayor of Peoria, Illinois had a number of very cute daughters. I, being the hormonal pre-teen that I was, fancied the daughter closest to my age. I still remember hanging out with her at SeaWorld and making out with her on the bus on the way back to the hotel. She actually was a year or so older than I was, which made it even more impressive. Anyway, I think I was focusing more on her than on my younger sister, who missed the bus back because she was apparently lost somewhere at SeaWorld that day. I obviously didn't seem too concerned.

These conferences also provided unique opportunities to meet some very important people with whom I would not typically rub shoulders. So in those early years, I began assembling autographs of those I perceived as famous people.

At one of the conferences, the city of Oakland, California sent a contingent of officials, including the mayor and a

George and Ruthie with children from Tondabayashi

host of vice-mayors. I got autographs from them all, and they convinced me to be an Oakland A's fan. This was during the A's amazing dominance in the American League and, although forever a Phillies and National League guy, I did spend about ten years tracking the A's.

Japan

The most unique travel experience, perhaps in my lifetime, was traveling to Bethlehem's Sister City, Tondabayashi, Japan.

Included in this trip was a stop-off in Hawaii each way to break up the trip. Poor us. We just couldn't imagine having to travel all that way without a break. So it certainly made sense to stop and sit in the sun and swim and relax for a couple of days on our way to and from Japan.

We made the most of the visit to Japan as well, spending time in both Tokyo and Osaka before arriving in Tondabayashi.

While there, when we traveled, we did so in a motorcade. My dad and the Tondabayashi mayor traveled in the first car. My mom and the mayor's wife were in the second car. Finally, my sister Ruthie and I were in the third car. In our car there was no interpreter, so no way to communicate with the others riding with us. I remember wanting to test this with my own pre-teen vocabulary, so I tried uttering some of the foulest words I could think of, just to see if I got any looks of disapproval from the others in the car. There was nothing but a few laughs from my sister.

Then there was the dinner at the mayor's house. He had a son who was around my age. While the dignitaries talked and ate and schmoozed inside, we hung out in his garage playing ping-pong and riding bikes around the alleys of his neighborhood. Although he spoke no English whatsoever, we got along amazingly.

At that point in my life, I think I had taken a couple years of piano lessons. I was finally beginning to use two hands when I played. However, I wasn't setting the world on fire with my abilities. Anyway, I had learned (at my parents' urging) how to play the Japanese folk song *"Sakura"* or "Cherry Blossoms." So everywhere we went that had a piano, my Dad would let everyone know I could play that song. Sure enough, I had a number of audiences of thirty-plus people cheering me on playing that song, which was like "Row, Row, Row Your Boat" here in the U.S.

Other Benefits

Phillies

In those days, the Philadelphia Phillies organization gave the mayor of Bethlehem complimentary season tickets. They weren't for a specific set of seats. Rather,

I loved throwing out the first pitch at Phillies games. Paul Marcincin is just to my right; his daughter's friend who was hit with the ball may be at the far right of the picture.

my dad could go to any game and show his pass, and they would give us four tickets to that game. Although we never knew where our seats would be, and often they were not great seats, we did end up going to a number of games over those years. It was special, because it was some good quality time with my dad.

In addition, every year they would have Bethlehem Day at Veterans Stadium. Of course, the mayor was the one who got to throw the first ball out for the game. This benefit got me amazing access to my favorite players from my favorite team, the likes of Bob Boone, Dave Cash, and Greg Luzinski.

One year, my friend Jeff Scheck and I actually got to walk down into the dugout. I remember seeing Dick Allen and Greg Luzinski sitting there before the game. Of course we said "Hi Dick, hi Greg." Neither guy looked terribly thrilled to see us. The only one who responded favorably was Bob Boone, who let us have our picture taken with him.

There was also the Bethlehem Day when Paul Marcincin joined us, along with his daughter and one of her friends. During warm-up, a ball was overthrown by one of the infielders and it flew over the head of Tony Taylor, the first baseman, and into the box seat where we sat. It hit Mary Beth Marcincin's friend on the head. The next thing I remember was Tony Taylor, Dave Cash, and Larry Bowa hovering over me, trying to get to the injured friend to make sure she was alright. She was and so was I.

One of the physical treasures I got out of my Phillies experience was my autographed baseball. One of the stadium ushers took a ball I had and brought it to the dugout. That ball got passed from one player to the next and from the Phillies dugout to the visiting team's dugout (the Montreal Expos). I ended up getting a baseball filled with an amazing potpourri of signatures that day. I still have the baseball, but the unfortunate thing is, no matter what I did to protect it, the signatures have faded to being almost unreadable. The memory and the bragging rights have never faded, though.

The People I got to Meet

In addition to the Phillies and the Tondabayashi mayor's son, I had the opportunity to meet some other impressive people.

There was Jimmy Carter. While my dad was mayor, Carter was running for president and his campaign brought him to the Lehigh Valley for a dinner fund-raising event. Since Jimmy was sitting right behind us (all we had to do was stand up and turn around and we were face-to-face with him) my dad took the opportunity to introduce me to him. After some brief pleasantries, I handed Jimmy a campaign brochure for an autograph. He wrote: "George, your father is very proud of you. Your friend, Jimmy Carter." Nice.

Henry Aaron also found his way to town for some promotional event. My father, being the not-so-shy guy that he is, got us in to see Henry before the masses ascended into wherever we were. So I had a few minutes to meet him and gain another impressive autograph in my ever-growing collection.

Perhaps the most impressive autograph for me was one I got from Mayor Tom Bradley, the first and only African-American mayor of Los Angeles. I met him at a reception at one of those mayors' conferences in San Juan, Puerto Rico. I was impressed enough to go up to him and not only ask for his autograph, but tell him that I had been learning about him from my social studies book in school.

Police Department – Impressing My Friends

As a young boy, I was particularly in awe of the police. I actually think, at that time, I wanted to be a police officer when I grew up. I was a huge fan of Joe Friday and *Dragnet*. I had a fake badge and had the Miranda Rights speech memorized and loved practicing, "You have the right to remain silent, any word you say can and will be used against you . . ."

There was not much impressive about City Hall, but one of the things I loved was the police department. In an effort to impress my friends, I would beg my dad to let me bring them there to see things that most people do not (thankfully) ever get to see. We would do things like go into the jail cell, the firing range and the communications center. We would ask whoever was on duty to take the fingerprints of my friends. Quite cool!

The city gave my dad a car during his four years. The car was equipped with a police radio, a spotlight, and a siren. It was fascinating listening to the police radio. I had the different police codes for various crimes memorized.

Every once in a while my dad would use the siren. If he would see a kid on a bicycle riding the wrong way on the street or something, he would blow his siren and scare the crap out of the kid and let him off with a warning never to ride his bike on the wrong side again.

Finally, there was the occasion of riding in a police car. Every once in a while, on a warm Friday night, my dad would ride along with a police officer for his shift, to get an idea of the kind of police matters that would happen on a given Friday evening. Occasionally I got to ride along, too. Unfortunately, I don't remember anything too wild or exciting except for a few domestic disturbances and some traffic-related violations.

The Tougher Stuff

Not Everyone Liked My Dad

As much as there was a load of great memories and benefits to being the mayor's son, there were also a number of difficult situations as well. I learned quickly that not everyone liked my dad. I learned that it is impossible, no matter how hard you try, to please everyone. My dad made a few people mad over the years. I knew he was not trying to win a popularity contest, but rather he was doing what he thought was right. He felt so strongly about this that it likely cost him his re-election bid.

This was hard for me. It was hard reading negative stuff about him in the newspaper. It was tough getting phone calls from people telling ME that my father was no good. Frankly, I was scarred by those calls. Even to this day, confrontation is hard for me. Even to this day, I try hard to please everyone because I didn't like the alternatives.

It was during those years that we got a second phone line into our house. No longer did Ruthie or I answer that main number. When there were events where the public knew my dad would be out, he would occasionally have a police car parked by our house watching, in the event of something suspicious happening.

I specifically remember his inauguration day and the dinner and dance that night. Apparently my sister and I were old enough to stay home alone. However, we still needed a police car posted outside, watching over the house. Ruthie and I were a little freaked out by the whole thing. I remember being convinced that something was going to happen that night. I remember tucking my toy (although it looked very real) gun into my back pocket in case I needed it. Sometime during the evening, the doorbell rang and there was an unfamiliar man at the front door. I was a little confused that this did not seem suspicious to the police, but nonetheless I answered the door with my toy gun drawn in my unexposed hand and ready to use, if necessary. As it turned out, it was a cab driver delivering a telegram of congratulations to my dad. Apparently in those days, cab drivers delivered telegrams. The good news was that I didn't have to use my weapon.

Quality Time vs. Quantity Time

My dad has been a great dad, before, during and after his years as mayor. Unfortunately during those years as mayor, the quantity of time I spent with him decreased. However, when he was present for my sisters and I, he was really present. We had a quality relationship with him.

I have already mentioned his intentionality with taking us to Phillies games. Also, during that time of our lives, we had a place in the Poconos. As a family, we went up there most weekends. It was our way of escaping life in Bethlehem for a couple of days and having some sense of being a real family together. We would often drive up there late on a Friday night, after my dad would have attended an event. He would then often drive home late Saturday afternoon for an event Saturday night. He would then drive back late that night, for the balance of the weekend.

So although he wasn't around us a lot, when he was around, he was really present in our lives.

The Elections

Interestingly, as I think back on the elections, I don't have as many memories of the elections my dad won. Rather the ones that stand out are the ones that he lost, two in particular.

General Election – 1969

This was his first attempt at being elected mayor. He won the primary and now was going up against the popular H. Gordon Payrow, who was running for his third term as mayor.

Apparently Mayor Payrow had a lot of friends at Spring Garden Elementary School. In fact, he had a lot of friends on my school bus as well. Since I was only in first grade, I hadn't developed many friendships yet. Kids back in those days must have been more politically-minded than they are now. Anyway, I think those kids at school and on my bus were taking out some of their political frustrations on me, as I would often get taunted for being Gordon Mowrer's son. Perhaps it didn't happen much, but as a six-year-old, it seemed like it happened every day through that election.

Then to top it off, my dad lost the election and I had to face those kids with that reality. So as a young man, I somehow mustered up an attitude of grace and told my dad that I was going to go up to those kids, and when they said something to me about my dad, I was going to say to them, "Rah rah for Payrow!" It was my introduction to the painful side of politics.

Primary Election – 1977

This time it's Mayor Mowrer running against City Council President Paul Marcincin. I'm now at Northeast Junior High School and Paul Marcincin had not only been my teacher a year earlier, but he was one of the most popular teachers at Northeast. I'm now eight years older and a little cockier than at Spring Garden, so I could hold my own to a certain degree. However, junior high school was tough and so were many of the kids.

My dad was a relatively popular mayor and would probably easily get re-elected. Or so I thought. I think we all were in shock as the results started coming into Mowrer Headquarters that night and the news was not good. My dad was on his way to one of the most difficult defeats of his life and in our family's life.

It didn't take long that night for my dad and his campaign team to realize that the election was over. It was time to drive from his headquarters on West Broad Street over to Marcincin Headquarters on East Broad Street. In the midst of my father's pain, he felt it appropriate to go over and congratulate Paul Marcincin face to face. For whatever reason, my dad asked if I wanted to go along. In my grief, I said yes.

We pulled into the parking lot and got out of the car. There was excitement and people pouring in and out of the entrance to the headquarters. Word spread that we had arrived. Paul Marcincin came out to greet us. In the midst of the hand-shaking and picture-taking and congratulations-making going on, Mayor-Elect Marcincin spotted me standing in the parking lot, left his festivities and came over to me. He took me away from the crowd and put his arm around me and he said, "George, in anything, there is a winner and a loser. Tonight I was the winner and your dad lost. That doesn't mean your dad is a bad person, because he is not."

As the tears came down my cheeks, he went on to say, "Tomorrow when you are in school, if anyone gives you a hard time about this or says anything mean to you, you come and tell me and I will take care of them."

As I write this, not only do the tears come back, but I also am reminded that it was less than a month ago that

Paul Marcincin passed away. Regardless of what kind of teacher or what kind of city councilman or what kind of mayor he was, more than anything that night, he won a lot of respect from me for leaving his party to console me. Thanks, Paul.

Conclusion

Those four years were pretty amazing. Overall they were loaded with extraordinary times and fantastic memories. I look back at them, and vividly remember them with great fondness, and as blessings that in one way or another have shaped and impacted me in profound ways.

Ruthie's Perspective

Here is the story of how nepotism let me down. It was the summer of 1987, it was the summer between my junior year of college and my senior year. I had broken my foot that spring. My intentions were to be a waitress at the shore, but because I could not be on my feet that much, I didn't have that as an option. So my father came to me and he said, "I have the perfect job for you, working for the health department in weed control." Essentially, this job was following through on complaints that were made to the City health department for garbage problems, garbage that had been left, dumping, for tall grass, for animal feces, for rat infestations and mice infestations. For any of the complaints that had been made to the health department, someone needed to go out to the property and confirm that there was indeed an issue, then go back and check city records, find out who the owner of the property was, and then send out citations.

There was a big huge deal about my taking this job, with an article written in the newspaper about nepotism, and all I could think was, "Who would actually *want* this job?" Very clearly, they couldn't find anybody else for the job. I'm pretty sure the pay was minimum wage, but I had the "thrill" of having this job.

While I worked in weed control for the City of Bethlehem, they gave me a car. I don't even know what kind of car it was, but it was painted red, an old patrol car for the fire department. It had two seats, one very large seat in the front and one very large seat in the back. And I had a police radio.

Something that made my day a little bit nicer was bringing my music box that played cassette tapes, and I would listen to my music as I would go around and follow up on these complaints. One day I was driving around, listening to my music, windows down, singing at the top of my lungs, and I found that there were some police cars that were following me. They pulled me over and let me know that my police radio was stuck open, and that I had been serenading everyone. No messages had gotten through, so they had to hunt me down and "unstick" my radio. That was one of the humiliating moments when I worked for the City of Bethlehem, in my "fabulous" job that my father, the Mayor of Bethlehem, had gotten me.

I used to go around to the properties, verify the problem, and go get my information from City Hall. Then I would go back to my little house on Main Street, which I shared with my friends from Moravian College, and I would watch soap operas while I wrote up my citations. I don't know if that was legitimate or not, but I used to do that. That's one of my confessions. This job was definitely a wonderful experience of being a "child of privilege."

My next story is about my relationship with the mayor of Tondabayashi, Japan. In 1974, the mayor came to visit us and stayed in our home. Any time we would have a houseguest, it seemed that my room was the room that we would put the guest in, and I would sleep in my brother's room. He had bunk beds, so I would move to his room and we would both sleep there. Every night, I would get up and go to the bathroom in the middle of the night.

One fine summer evening, I got up to use the toilet in the middle of the night, and being half asleep, or mostly asleep, I made my way back to my room and crawled in bed. When I woke up in the morning, I was absolutely horrified to see that I had crawled in bed with the mayor of Tondabayashi, Japan. I can't even imagine what he was thinking, but I nearly crawled out of my skin. I got out of bed immediately, went tearing into my parents' room, and said to my father, "That was the most horrible joke you could possibly play on me, putting me in bed with him." And he, of course, just started to laugh, because he hadn't done it, I had done it myself. But to this day I enjoy telling people that I slept with the mayor of Tondabayashi, Japan. Enough said.

In all the years of my father's political involvement, he was a very, very busy man. He had lots of meetings and appointments, and he was not home very much, although he was home for dinner most nights. But in all of his busyness, one of the things that he went out of his way to impress upon his family was, "If you ever need me, I will be there for you. All you need to do is make it known." So if I would need to talk to him at any point, I would just call his office and they would put me through, whether he was in a conference or not. He was always accessible.

When he was interim mayor in 1987, I was a student at Moravian College, and lived on the South Campus, on Church Street in Main Hall. One spring morning, it was my birthday, and since it was a warmer April, we had the windows of our dorm room open. I woke up to the sound of my father serenading me, singing "Happy Birthday." He wasn't just singing "Happy Birthday" to me, he was serenading the whole of Main Hall in all of his glory, with his beautiful singing voice. He has always been a performer. And as he sang to me, once again, I was horrified; I was completely embarrassed. But it was really neat because people came to me throughout the day and said, "Your father is so cute. That was the sweetest thing. I can't even imagine that my father would do something like that." Having the convenience of my father being in City Hall, right up the street, and expressing in this act that even though there were many pressing issues in his life, that with all of that, I still was important and significant enough for him to come down and sing this song, even though at the time I felt a little self-conscious about the act, it was still really special. I can look back and just smile at how very loving and tender this man of "prestige" really was.

Gordon on Ruthie

When we went to the U.S. Conference of Mayors convention in California, we went to SeaWorld. (George remembered this, too.) At various times, you would hear some of the mayors being paged over the loudspeaker system, like the mayor of Los Angeles, Mayor Bradley, or the mayor of New York. You assumed that they were being called for an important message from their office. One time Mayor Mowrer from Bethlehem was paged: it seems that his daughter was lost. Even though children were not

Meg Mowrer, learning the political ropes early

In 1977, the Bethlehem Christmas lights were turned on by Meg Mowrer, 5, and David Scholl, 6. *Courtesy the Express-Times*

normally allowed with the mayors' party, Ruthie had been allowed to come to SeaWorld with all of the mayors. Ruthie got lost in SeaWorld.

Gordon on Meg

Meg missed out on a lot when I was mayor the first time, because she was so young, and she does not remember much. She did get to help me turn on the official Bethlehem Christmas lights in 1977. When I was mayor in 1987, however, she was old enough to be involved more.

Gordon on his Family

My family was always a part of my life when I was mayor, and I was always proud of them. We did many activities together. We had fun and we accepted our role seriously. Today we have good memories and are willing to share them.

The Globe-Times

'Maintaining the People's Right to Know'

Page 6   Friday, December 30, 1977

*One must not always think so much about what one
should do, but rather what one should be. Our works do
not ennoble us; but we must ennoble our works.*
—*Meister Eckhart*

The Mowrer Years

Gordon Mowrer, who ends his first and only term as mayor of Bethlehem this week, can take his leave of City Hall knowing that achievements in office temper his personal disappointment. While the mayor could not win re-election in his party's primary, even those who worked for his defeat must admit he has won the appreciation of citizens in important ways.

Mayor Mowrer was philosophically a good leader. He sought to give the city a positive, progressive spirit. He set a high personal example of honesty and accessibility in office. His respect for the people's right to know can be viewed as a model for any government.

One of the ironies of his defeat is that the good things he fought for probably will not be visible until long after he is out of office. He was blamed when the city's grand downtown plans were blown apart by a recession and court suits, which discouraged would-be developers. Yet, he did his best to break the city away from the yoke of the Redevelopment Authority's Clarke and Rapuano planning designs when their directions no longer seemed in the city's best interests.

The mayor probably paid politically for his frustrated attempt to fire the redevelopment authority executive director, a recalcitrant of the bulldozing age whose time has passed. To this day, he has probably never received full credit for trying to steer the city towards rehabilitation and away from demolition.

It was not until he already had been defeated that Mowrer realized his ambition to spare Main Street the problems of Broad. When earth was broken earlier this month for the project to restore Main St. to its Victorian heritage, it was a satisfying affirmation that he had swung the city toward a more credible policy of revitalization.

The breakthrough could not have occurred without Mowrer's vigorous and imaginative drive to pursue federal and state funds for Bethlehem. Well before other cities had even gotten into line, Mowrer had plans ready for consideration as public projects under the Public Works Employment Act of 1976. That he won $2.5 million for the city — after the primary election — did not help him politically, but it was a triumph for the city.

This sheer persistence in chasing dollars being distributed in Washington explains how Bethlehem was able to put up over $1 million as a primer for Main St. restoration. That is how the city will get a $2.2 million maintenance garage. And that is how the Bethlehem Area School District will find $48,671 to restore its building front in the Main St. revitalization.

The mayor can take much credit for the apartments for the elderly going up on the South Side — about the only public improvement to rise in the bulldozed spaces of this embattled neighborhood in 20 years. The city's improved anti-crime effort can be traced to the team policing concept launched under the Mowrer administration. His program to enlarge and diversify public recreational facilities leaves Bethlehem with leisure opportunities unequaled in any other Pennsylvania city of this size.

It is not the purpose here to weigh the Mowrer contributions against his mistakes in office or indiscretions of those in his administration, even if it were possible to fathom the perplexities of Bethlehem politics which brought his defeat. We are certain only that he leaves the incoming mayor, Paul Marcincin, a city with strong resources.

Gordon Mowrer gave to his office all that was in him. And that's all taxpayers had a right to expect.

13

The Mowrer Years

As I was leaving office at the end of 1977, the *Bethlehem Globe-Times* published an editorial about my term. I think it sums up my four-year term pretty well. It is reprinted here, with the permission of the *Express-Times*, as it appeared on December 30, 1977.

The Mowrer Years

Gordon Mowrer, who ends his first and only term as mayor of Bethlehem this week, can take his leave of City Hall knowing that achievements in office temper his personal disappointment. While the mayor could not win re-election in his party's primary, even those who worked for his defeat must admit he has won the appreciation of citizens in important ways.

Mayor Mowrer was philosophically a good leader. He sought to give the city a positive, progressive spirit. He set a high personal example of honesty and accessibility in office. His respect for the people's right to know can be viewed as a model for any government.

One of the ironies of his defeat is that the good things he fought for probably will not be visible until long after he is out of office. He was blamed when the city's grand downtown plans were blown apart by a recession and court suits, which discouraged would-be developers. Yet, he did his best to break the city away from the yoke of the Redevelopment Authority's Clarke and Rapuano planning designs when their directions no longer seemed in the city's best interests.

The mayor probably paid politically for his frustrated attempt to fire the redevelopment authority executive director, a recalcitrant of the bulldozing age whose time has passed. To this day, he has probably never received full credit for trying to steer the city towards rehabilitation and away from demolition.

It was not until he already had been defeated that Mowrer realized his ambition to spare Main Street the problems of Broad. When earth was broken earlier this month for the project to restore Main St. to its Victorian heritage, it was a satisfying affirmation that he had swung the city toward a more credible policy of revitalization.

The breakthrough could not have occurred without Mowrer's vigorous and imaginative drive to pursue federal and state funds for Bethlehem. Well before other cities had even gotten into line, Mowrer had plans ready for consideration as public projects under the Public Works Employment Act of 1976. That he won $2.5 million for the city – after the primary election – did not help him politically, but it was a triumph for the city.

This sheer persistence in chasing dollars being distributed in Washington explains how Bethlehem was able to put up over $1 million as a primer for Main St. restoration. That is how the city will get a $2.2 million maintenance garage. And that is how the Bethlehem Area

School District will find $48,671 to restore its building front in the Main St. revitalization.

The mayor can take much credit for the apartments for the elderly going up on the South Side – about the only public improvement to rise in the bulldozed spaces of this embattled neighborhood in 20 years. The city's improved anti-crime effort can be traced to the team policing concept launched under the Mowrer administration. His program to enlarge and diversify public recreational facilities leaves Bethlehem with leisure opportunities unequaled in any other Pennsylvania city of this size.

It is not the purpose here to weigh the Mowrer contributions against his mistakes in office or indiscretions of those in his administration, even if it were possible to fathom the perplexities of Bethlehem politics which brought his defeat. We are certain only that he leaves the incoming mayor, Paul Marcincin, a city with strong resources.

Gordon Mowrer gave to his office all that was in him. And that's all taxpayers had a right to expect.

Chapter

14

Final Thoughts

As I look back at my memories of my time at City Hall, I ask myself what the most significant things that happened to me were, how did they affect my life, and what does it mean to me today? One word that comes to mind is "variety," especially the variety of people I was privileged to meet.

I feel very fortunate to have had the incredible experience of meeting with so many different kinds of people. Being able to take time to sit and listen to people on a Wednesday afternoon at Open Door, people who wanted to come in and see the mayor, whether they were rich or poor, young or old, "important" or Mr. Average Joe on the street, was a wonderful experience for me, and I look back on it as a great privilege. I met so many different kinds of people in that office, from ordinary citizens of Bethlehem to department heads and local leaders to people of national prominence, such as legislators, governors of the state of Pennsylvania, and presidents of the United States.

I think not only of my visit with Jimmy Carter in the Oval Office when he was president, but I think also of the first time I spent some time with Jimmy Carter. When he was running for president, he came to the Lehigh Valley to speak and to campaign at the gates of Bethlehem Steel. I met him at the airport, and was asked to introduce him for a press conference. In those days, after you held a press conference, you had to wait for an hour before you could go out and do your speaking engagements. So Jimmy Carter and I sat in a broom closet, the janitors' unit, in the airport for that hour and we talked. I asked him all kinds of questions and he responded to me very methodically. For everything that I asked him, he had an answer. What impressed me most about that is later during his campaign when I heard him speak on television, if people would ask him a similar question, Jimmy gave an answer that was very consistent with the one he gave when he was alone with me. It was then that I realized his mind had been mentally programmed to give the same answer to questions, so that people could not accuse him of changing his mind. I was impressed with that process.

I also spent time with several governors of the commonwealth of Pennsylvania. During one difficult time for Bethlehem Steel, Governor Casey was coming to Bethlehem to encourage government to help the steel industry. For that particular event, he arrived over an hour early. That was almost unheard of, when it came to somebody like the president or the governor. They almost always came late, and you almost always waited for them. But Bob Casey sat in my office for almost an hour as we talked about all kinds of things related to politics and government and his future. Senator Reibman had joined us for that event, and we just relaxed and talked. I also had opportunities to meet with Governor Milton Shapp, both in his office and also in my office when he came to town to see what was going on in Bethlehem.

I am also grateful for the relationship that I had with Fred B. Rooney, Bethlehem's congressman while I was mayor. Fred's wife was a girlhood friend of my wife, many years ago before either couple was married. Fred worked with me to run my first campaign for mayor. When I took my family to visit Washington, he made the arrangements for my family to go through the White House, the FBI building, the Air and Space Museum, the Treasury Building, and other facilities. He took us to the congressional dining room for lunch, and even took our daughter Ruthie down to where he sat and where he voted, and showed her how that happened. He went the extra mile and was very gracious to us. We always had a good relationship, so I say thank you to Fred B. Rooney, our congressman. I am delighted that one of the high-rise buildings that I helped bring to Bethlehem is named in his honor, The Fred B. Rooney Building on the South Side of Bethlehem.

As mayor of Bethlehem, attending the National League of Cities and U.S. Conference of Mayors conventions, I got to meet all kinds of elected officials throughout the United States. What impressed me most about the elected officials is that almost everyone I met was sincere and honest in their endeavors and really wanted to do what was right for their community and for the people who had elected them. I was also impressed with their spirituality. In fact, when I attended the National League of Cities convention, I noticed they had no prayer breakfast or spiritual breakfast. I suggested it to the planners, and they said no one would come if they had one. I encouraged them to give it a try, and they asked me to suggest a speaker. I said that the first year I would ask Robert Schuller, the head of the Crystal Cathedral in California, and they said, "Who's he?" He was nationally celebrated, and has been ever since; he operates a very successful church and ministry, including training pastors. I made the contact with him, he agreed to come, and the breakfast was sold out before the convention even opened. Ever since that time, they have been holding a prayer breakfast at the National League of Cities conventions.

I was very impressed with all of the elected officials that I worked with, and how much they cared, but sometimes I wonder, "What happened?" Sometimes I think that whenever we give someone a lot of power, as they say, "Power corrupts, and absolute power corrupts absolutely." So often elected officials have the feeling that they are really important because they are treated like they are important. One time my wife and I went to a dinner that the Puerto Rican community held on the South Side. When I walked in the door, someone came up to me and said, "Oh, you're Mayor Mowrer, you sit here in front." They treated me like I was royalty. It is a nice feeling when people treat you well, but elected officials need to remember that the feeling is often not for them personally, but rather a feeling of respect for the elected position that they hold.

Perhaps the idea that remains with me most about this variety and number of people that I have met and dealt with is that everybody, regardless of who they are or where they come from, is basically alike. All these folks have

a) feelings, they all care, they are all sensitive

b) personal, family and community lives

c) secrets, are struggling in some way, and keep a lot to themselves

But we are all alike, and that is really very significant. If you understand that, then it is much easier to deal with people and love them and care for them. That, of course, was ultimately my goal.

We ran into the same variety of people when we walked the streets in Bethlehem's neighborhoods and listened to people express their issues and mention problems which concerned them. We dealt with an impressive variety of issues while I was mayor: the landfill, the parks and public property, overlay of streets, financial matters, recycling issues, housing for senior citizens, housing for the poor, it was tremendously interesting. There were the problems that each of the departments handled, things like drug abuse or fire inspections, financial matters and the bonds that the city needed to buy, developments in computers and technology. It was a wide variety of issues.

It was incredible training for my later life when I became a minister. The issues and the varieties of people that I dealt with at City Hall were related to the issues and the varieties of people that I would be dealing with in a church. Whether you are in government or in business or in ministry, many of the same problems and issues occur. So I was able to take my administrative and business experience from before I was mayor, and my mayor's experience with all of those issues, and apply them to my congregation, so that I was able to do a much better job. The experiences at City Hall made a significant difference to the rest of my life, and I look back with positive feelings.

The foundation of everything I did was my faith. When I was mayor I would start each day in the office with a half hour of quiet. From 8:00 to 8:30 no one would disturb me. I would read one chapter from a Bible given to me by my brother and his wife (I completely read it from the beginning to the end during my time there). I would take twenty minutes to meditate (transcendental meditation, or "TM," was big in those days). Then thanking God for that day, I would ask for His presence and guidance and pray for that day's events. I was then ready to go. It was 8:30 a.m. and City Hall would come alive!

Serving as mayor was a wonderful experience. So when I look back I say, "Thank you, Bethlehem," for the opportunity of getting to know such a variety of people, the chance to touch base with such a variety of issues, and the privilege of serving you.

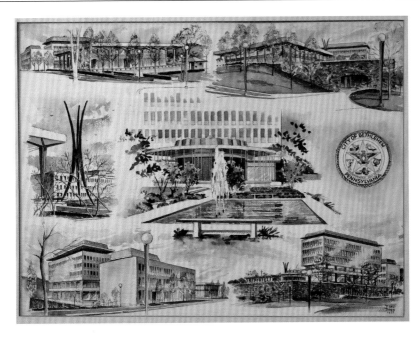

When I left office in 1977, I was presented with two paintings by Bethlehem artist Fred Bees, one of views of City Hall and the surrounding plaza, and one of some of Bethlehem's historic Moravian buildings.

Afterword

That so much has been said about Gordon Brown Mowrer is no surprise. The man whose stories, experiences, and wisdom are contained within this book is more than just a sum total of these stories. He is my grandfather, and the Gordon that I know is "Papa," a man not of the political years but of the years after his final term as mayor. I know him as a pastor, as an aging city councilman fighting to preserve Bethlehem's dignity, as a man who loves his wife, children, and grandchildren. I know him most of all as a man who refuses to turn away and give up – from demanding, at restaurants, for his food be cooked up to *his* standards (petty, humorous) to fighting major physical ailments for nearly the last quarter century of his life (profound, moving).

This is, however, the grandfather I have already known. In reading the stories presented here in this book, I have grown to know better the man who has meant so much to so many different people. Unlike my grandmother, aunts, and father, I do not have memories of him as mayor to share. What I hope to offer instead is a sense of order to these stories that Gordon Mowrer shares so easily. It is through the sharing and understanding of memories that their true value is found; these are not some dusty old stories of small-town Americana duty, but rather the care and the love of a man who was passionate about what he did. I hope that by naming and describing the following themes, the values important to my grandfather, shared through his memories, will become clear and meaningful.

I. Tradition

Respect for those who have gone before us is one of the central tenets of my grandfather's life, not only throughout his time in public service, but before and after as well. It has been made apparent in the simple act of writing this book. *He has stories to tell.* His are stories that are not just about him, but stories that involve people who are protagonists or antagonists – people who have affected him. Through the telling of these stories, he honors those who have had an impact on him.

Tradition has also had an impact on his public policy. In reading about his first term as mayor and his championing the use of preexisting buildings to remind both resident and visitor alike of Bethlehem's rich past and its legacy in the Lehigh Valley, I am reminded, ironically, of his latest fight for tradition and history in Bethlehem. The public policy *I* will always associate with Gordon Mowrer is his fight against the introduction of gambling into the city of Bethlehem. As a politically idealistic high school senior at that time, I could not have sided more wholly with him nor been more proud to be related to the 70-year-old Moravian pastor taking on the whole Sands Corporation. Although the dust has settled and the lights of the casino illuminate the city today, I have been permanently moved by that fight and the message that was rooted within it: that Bethlehem has more to offer than cheap thrills. Ours is a city built by loving people of faith, and to take that for granted is to ignore the very reason that this city exists.

II. Love

This leads beautifully into the second theme I have noticed throughout these stories. My grandfather is a loving man. He is a man who has come in contact with nearly every possible kind of person and looks for the good in them all. He is a man who will insist, after meeting any one of these people, that we are all the same; that we are all really one human race. After that obvious eye-rolling and uttering of "batty old man," the truth of his words cannot, by any stretch of the imagination, be ignored. He is correct. We are really not so different from each other that there should be anything that remains between us other than love.

My sister and I were recently discussing the importance of love and how it can too easily be spurned for the call of power. Despite having been a man "in power," my grandfather made love the driving factor of his years as mayor. His actions and efforts as mayor or as councilman were not a quest to rule Bethlehem, but rather to work for its benefit with those who worked for him. Together, with the common goal of service rather than rule, love has provided the driving force behind not just his days in office but also his time as a pastor, as a community-oriented small businessman, and as a family man.

III. Persistence

The question I asked myself after reading through the memories naturally concerned his defeat by Paul Marcincin in 1977. Why, after his successful term as a young, energetic mayor, did Gordon Mowrer lose? Not exactly afraid to bring it up but certainly not wanting to be the first to jump into the topic, I waited until he brought up the loss. No doubt my grandfather had developed his own theories in the thirty-plus years since that election. And he has. In a moment, everything that he had accomplished was distilled into a simple idea: persistence.

He lost in 1977 so he could be appointed in 1987 and receive the hero's welcome back into office that he did. His loss did not mean that it was over, but rather that his course had been altered. Similarly, my grandfather failed out of his first semester at Dickinson College so he could come back and graduate successfully, having touched the hearts and minds of at least a few during his time there. The reason he has been challenged with anything throughout his life is exactly for that reason: so he could be challenged. As a young child first not expected to survive his neo-natal hospital care, then not expected to move past fifth grade, graduate high school, etc., he has been coming back his whole life, seizing greater opportunity created out of initial failure and creating success where, to most, there would only be disappointment.

One final story that is particularly poignant, perhaps equally as poignant as the story my father shared of that Election Day in 1977, is the story of my grandfather's first loss in a mayoral campaign, to Gordon Payrow, in 1969. Having lost the election, the young Gordon Mowrer decided to go to the victor, the older Gordon Payrow, who was on that night celebrating in the Hotel Bethlehem. As my grandfather entered the main hall, he was booed by Payrow's supporters, and obviously, the majority of those in attendance were supporting the elder Gordon. To be booed by a room (and a large and elegant one, at that) filled with people must have been a terrifying and formative experience. I wince at the slight thought that someone could be less than pleased with me; to be confronted with such volume of opposition would certainly send me to the floor. And yet my grandfather came to congratulate Gordon Payrow (who called, of course, for order and an end to the booing) and did so, and had the tenacity to move forward from a potentially traumatic experience and run again for mayor. Comeback Kid, indeed.

In a final note, I would also like to point out that Gordon Mowrer has been recently diagnosed with Parkinson's disease. Amid worries and unknown fears of how this diagnosis will affect him, my grandfather has been, in the past months, not quite himself. Yet he called me excitedly this week with a revelation after reading the memoirs of the actor Michael J. Fox. Through reading, he was reminded of the important role his persistence plays in our lives and proceeded, over the phone, to explain his newfound hope despite the insecurity of the diagnosis. I can only attempt to explain how relieving this was for me. Gordon Mowrer has a lot of life ahead of him and a lot more stories to tell. Of that, I am sure.

Richard Gordon Mowrer
January, 2010

Appendixes

Bethlehem Mayors

Name	in Office	Born	Died	Age at First Election
Archibald Johnston	1918-1922	May 30, 1864	Feb 1, 1948	53
James M. Yeakle	1922-1930	Mar 28, 1860	Dec 23, 1941	61
Robert Pfeifle	1930-1950	Apr 14, 1880	Mar 22, 1958	49
Earl E. Schaffer	1950-1962	Aug 5, 1902	Jun 11, 1982	47
H. Gordon Payrow	1962-1974	Feb 4, 1918	Apr 13, 2004	43
Gordon B. Mowrer	1974-1978	Feb 9, 1936	--	36
Paul M. Marcincin	1978-1987	Jun 20, 1921	Oct 26, 2009	56
Gordon B. Mowrer	1987-1988	(second time)	--	(50)
Kenneth R. Smith	1988-Sep 1997	1939	--	48
Paul M. Marcincin	Oct 1997- Jan 1998	(second time)	--	(76)
Donald T. Cunningham, Jr.	1998-Feb 2003	1965	--	31
Dennis W. Reichard	Feb-Mar 2003	1949	--	53
James A. Delgrosso	Mar-Dec 2003	Jun 30, 1943	Oct. 8, 2009	59
John Callahan	2004-	1969	--	34

(To preserve the privacy of mayors who were still living when this book was printed, only their birth year is shown.)

Highlights from the 1974 Mayor's Annual Report
(presented January 7, 1975)

I would like to take this opportunity to give members of council and citizens of Bethlehem my annual report on activities and programs of this administration in 1974, as well as give you a sense of where we are headed in future years.

1974 was my first year as Mayor, and we are proud of the strides made in several important areas; first, in the overall management of City Hall and second, in the development and improvement of the qualify of life in our community.

Management Improvements begun in 1974

Dissolution of the Department of Public Safety, separating Police and Fire into two departments

Establishment of Department of Community Development, to coordinate planning, inspections, health, Redevelopment Authority activities. With Franklin Gaugler as director, the department has done an outstanding job in coordinating numerous and diverse community development activities.

Establishment of Service & Information Office under the Mayor's direction, to handle citizen complaints and requests for services. The department will install a Centrex phone system in 1975 to further centralize the department, so that citizens have only one number to call for service and information (an integral part of efforts to make government more responsive and responsible to Bethlehem citizens).

New Management by Objectives (MBO) Concept requires city managerial personnel to develop specific goals and objectives to be accomplished by their department or bureau by specific dates. Preliminary results have been noticeable and encouraging; management has become proactive rather than crisis-oriented. With an IPA grant, Sam DeWald of Penn State has trained over 40 managerial personnel in MBO techniques.

Improvement of Productivity (increasing service while reducing manpower, finances, equipment, and materials needed): I have established a Management Team of the Mayor's Administrative Assistant, Daniel Fitzpatrick, Chair; Erma Aubert, Business Administrator; Norman Allan, Director of Budget and Finance. They will examine and analyze all city departments for effectiveness and efficiency; review all vacancies as they occur in 1975, review or establish other programs to promote productivity and performance.

Productivity will also be improved by utilizing more computers (a Computer Council has been established to present a five-year plan to increase the use of computers); reducing the number of city-owned vehicles; and adding no new personnel in 1975, instead improving the service of current employees.

Established Mayor's Commendation Award, to recognize employees who serve Bethlehem citizens beyond the normal call of duty.

Received Law Enforcement Assistance Administration (LEAA) Grant for MBO program to improve productivity in the Police Department.

Development and Improvement of Quality of Life

South Side: began comprehensive housing rehabilitation program, utilizing resources of the Department of Community Development and Housing Development Corporation, including allocating $250,000 for low-interest rehab loans and $100,000 for rehab grants. Program also includes improvement of streets, tree planting, improving utilities. Bethlehem was the first city in Pennsylvania to submit an application for Community Development Grant funds.

Funds also were earmarked for a Central Business District on Fourth Street, including clearing a site for a senior citizens high-rise building, in cooperation with the Housing Authority, and new commercial areas. Two new parks were begun on the South Side, to be completed in 1975, on property donated by the Bethlehem School District. Plans to apply for Federal grants for a swimming pool complex at Broughal Junior High School have begun. A bilingual social worker for the Southeast Neighborhood Center was hired to work with Spanish-speaking youths.

Downtown Renewal (North Side): ground has been broken for Bethlehem Plaza Mall, the new First Valley Bank building has been completed and occupied, school district offices have moved downtown. The new First Valley Bank ice rink and Family of Man sculpture bring enthusiasm and excitement to the downtown.

Downtown projects in the works: possibility of building a hotel-convention center complex and Performing Arts Center (state funds being sought); the city contributed $25,000 to assist the Sun Inn Preservation Association in purchasing the Sun Inn; city department is conducting a comprehensive study of the historical significance and possible architectural motifs of Main Street; a draft of an Urban Beautification study has been received.

Other projects: Westside Park construction begun, as well as a new park at the site of the former Higbee School; storm sewer program for Northeast Bethlehem begun.

Sister City commission: Mr. Sakon, from Tondabayashi, began construction of a Japanese Tea House in the Serenity Garden. Two firms cooperated in providing the copper roof for the tea house. The mayor of Tondabayashi visited Bethlehem.

Bethlehem Bicentennial Committee has been hard at work, preparing for the celebration in 1976.

Openness to Community: An Open Door Program has been established, where on any Wednesday any citizen can walk into the mayor's office, without an appointment, and discuss any concerns. Citizens have come in every Wednesday, with a high of 37 in one afternoon. Channel 39 and cable television services are also being used for presentations of what is going on in Bethlehem City Hall. At 12:10 every day, I host a talk show on WGPA radio. The press has been included or briefed on virtually every major topic of concern for Bethlehem and her citizens.

In closing, I must say that the Mayor and members of City Council have worked very closely together on issues of major concern and import to Bethlehem citizens, because we both have a sincere desire to make Bethlehem a better place to live. Through a continued cooperative and harmonious spirit, we can carry forward the necessary programs to make Bethlehem truly a model community.

Highlights from the 1975 Mayor's Annual Report

(published in the *Bethlehem Globe-Times,* February 9, 1976)

My message will outline the progress and problems of 1975 and the challenges and opportunities for 1976.

Management, Productivity, Fiscal Responsibility

Economic recession and spiraling inflation continue to plague all of us. As we attempt to balance municipal service needs with shrinking revenue we have adopted a policy, through Management By Objectives, of improving management in such a way that we are able to maintain our quality services with fewer inputs of manpower, equipment, and material. Programs which will be continued into 1976 include:

- Management training programs
- Systematic analysis and review of manpower needs
- Elimination of marginal or unnecessary programs
- Professional labor negotiations
- Programs paid by increased charges to users
- Purchasing used equipment, where practical, rather than new
- Using smaller cars and a comprehensive vehicle control system
- Selling of unnecessary buildings and property to put them on the tax roles, as well as to reduce operating and maintenance expenses
- The continuation of the Management By Objectives Program

Police Service

Unfortunately, 1975 saw crime in Bethlehem rise dramatically, but still well under national trends. Our emphasis, in 1976, will focus on:

- Better utilization of manpower . . . One possibility is the concept of Team Policing, where officers are returned to city neighborhoods on a regular basis and work with the citizens to control crime.
- Crime Prevention Programs

Fire Service

The Fire Department has expended a great deal of manpower in 1975 in preventive programs such as increased inspection and testing, and in the new ordinance requiring sprinklers in highrise buildings. The most disturbing factor of 1975 was the alarming rise in arsons and false alarms. Programming for 1976 will include:

- Increased inspections of commercial and industrial establishments
- Beginning of a home inspection program
- Removal of many fire alarm boxes (85% of our false alarms come in on alarm boxes)
- Training and equipping several officers in techniques of arson investigation and prosecution
- Continued updating of fire codes and ordinances, and the stringent enforcement of them

Community Development

Tremendous strides were made in 1975 for providing loan and grant programs for housing rehabilitation, the acquisition of a site for a highrise for the elderly, and the planning for Main Street restoration. But, the past year had its frustrations. Several lawsuits delayed downtown renewal and construction of the municipal parking garage. Fortunately, these suits have been successfully concluded and renewal projects will move forward.

Community Development projects for 1976 include:
- Central Business District Renewal
- Construction and opening of Walnut Street parking garage
- Opening of the Bethlehem Plaza Mall
- Construction and opening of the Broad Street pedestrian plaza and widening of Guetter Street to North Street
- Review of plans for a hotel/convention center complex and possible construction activity
- Completion of downtown mini-parks
- Continued efforts to attract new businesses to the downtown area
- Complete review and analysis of downtown renewal and revitalization efforts by an Urban Land Institute panel of professional planners
- Main Street Revitalization: presentation of plans
- Begin restoration of the Sun Inn
- South Side Central Business District
- The clearance of the southeastern block at Fourth and New Streets for construction of a 150-unit highrise for the elderly
- Housing Rehabilitation

Parks & Recreation

The year 1976 will see the completion of several neighborhood parks. We anticipate the construction of the first indoor-outdoor swimming pool complex at the Broughal Junior High School. Our philosophy is that users – not all property owners – should pay for services.

Public Works

A large portion of each year's capital budget is allocated to the Public Works Department for street, water, and sanitary and storm sewer construction or reconstruction. Due to austerity budgeting, these accounts have been substantially reduced. There will be funding in 1976 for a number of projects concerning the Waste Water Treatment Plant, reconstruction of streets, improvements to the city storm sewer in some areas, extention of sewers, and improvement of water quality and supply.

Citizen Access to Government

This administration has pledged itself to openness, honesty, and candor in our relationships with the people of Bethlehem and with the press. We have expanded our efforts to serve citizens with the establishment of a separate office and phone number for information, service and complaints. My open-door policy will continue as will my efforts to meet with numerous city organizations. It is appropriate to observe our nation's bicentennial . . . With our hiring of a full-time Bicentennial Coordinator, we will enjoy numerous special events to help celebrate our nation's 200th birthday and the special heritage which makes Bethlehem great.

The year 1976 is a year of challenge and opportunity. Only with your continued guidance and active participation can we truly realize our individual and collective dreams.

Highlights from the 1976 Mayor's Annual Report

(published in the *Bethlehem Globe-Times* March 28, 1977)

The year was special for our City primarily because we had the opportunity to celebrate our Bicentennial year with numerous "people events."

Many of the ideas which have come to fruition are a result of you, the people of Bethlehem. Many of these ideas came as a result of my Walking Tours through all parts of the City, a motorcycle trip through the public housing areas, as well as my continued Wednesday afternoon Open Door program, WGPA radio show, Channel 39 monthly TV specials, and cable shows.

★   Bicentennial Events – The Freedom Train, Heritage Happenings, July 4th Ecumenical Service, etc.

★   Neighborhood Team Policing reduces crime 23%

★   Fire False Alarms down 43%

★   Fire incidents reduced 58% primarily due to prevention programs

★   Public Works cut overtime 50%

★   Barriers removed to make City Hall accessible to the handicapped

★   New direction for Downtown-Main Street restoration planned

★   Resolved storm sewer problem in Northeast Bethlehem with retention program

★   800-car Parking Garage completed

★   Broad Street Pedestrian Mall completed

★   1.5 million dollars promised by Gov. Shapp for Civic-Human Resources Center

★   Site prepared for 4th & New Streets Senior Citizen Highrise and 15,000 sq. ft. of commercial area

★   Urban Land Institute study completed

★ $250,000 available from State for Broughal Pool

★   Mayor Mowrer selected Elected Official of Year in Penna. by Pennsylvania Planning Association

★   Higbee, Fairview and Packer Parks constructed, Friendship Park revitalized

★   Lehigh Canal completed and dedicated

★   New phone number for all City emergencies planned

★   Walking Tours throughout the City by Mayor and key staff members to learn citizen concerns

★   Major revitalization of Monocacy Creek banks begun

★   Municipal Enterprise System adopted

★   Redevelopment, Parking Authority, and Bethlehem Water Authority moved to City Hall

★   Camp Monocacy Summer Day Care Program became the first such camp in Pennsylvania

★   Department of Community Affairs grant, $100,000.00 for South Side rehab housing program

★   Six obsolete properties were razed

Also:

•   The Fire Department purchased a new 100-foot aerial truck and received a new fire pumper

•   The store fronts of Tom Bass, Bixler's and the Heritage set the mood downtown for other owners planning to fit in with the historic street-scape improvements

•   Historic building inventory submitted by Jim Ward – complete inventory with description, history, and pictures of all historic buildings in Bethlehem's Historic District

- The Broad Street Pedestrian Mall was completed and several store rentals were finalized for the Bethlehem Plaza Mall
- The Walnut Street Parking Garage was completed
- Restoration plans neared completion for the Sun Inn
- In the South Side Central Business District, clearance was completed of the southeastern block at Fourth and New Streets for construction of a 150-unit highrise for the elderly, complete with recreational facilities and street-level commercial establishments
- The construction of the Waste Water Treatment Plant expansion is 60% complete; grant money received so far for this project totals over $2.6 million

As we move into the Third Century of our nation's history, I ask for your continued support and cooperation, as only together can we accomplish good things for our City.

Highlights from the 1977 City of Bethlehem Annual Report

(presented December 30, 1977)

Long-awaited and much needed projects to benefit Bethlehem's citizens began in 1977, including the Main Street Program, three Senior Citizen Highrises, and the Municipal Service Center.

Main Street Program – sets a new direction for Downtown Bethlehem, an effort for the first time to revitalize our heritage rather than to replace it. It calls for the return of Victorian building facades, street lights of that period, slate sidewalks and the like. Building fronts from Church to Broad Streets are getting facelifts.

Senior Citizen Highrises – groundbreakings have taken place. The City was able to compete successfully for program assistance from the US Department of Housing and Urban Development (HUD) to provide 455 units at Moravian II and Lutheran Manor, as well as the Southside Highrise.

Municipal Services Garage – is under construction. The $1.86 million for construction was obtained from the Federal Public Works Grant. City Council provided an additional $265,238 so the project could be 100% complete.

Many Projects Completed

The Department of Parks and Public Property, with Charles Brown as Acting Director, has completed the nine-hole golf course and the driving range at the Illick's Mill complex, and business has been brisk. Our city parks have been upgraded and repaired, and new ones have been created. All are now in top shape. In Monocacy Park, repair work, including new wash structures, was finished.

Four new playgrounds were built from scratch at Elmwood, Fairview, Higbee and McNamara. Major renovations were made in 1977 to Bayard, Canal Towpath, Clearview, Heimple, Kings Mansion, Monocacy Fields, Saucon, the Rose Garden, the Sell complex, Ullmann, South Mountain, West Side and Yosko. At Sand Island, the tennis court building was completely remodeled.

This department, which includes the Recreation Bureau, also assisted at 25 major special events, including the Christmas City Fair, and at 60 events for Music in the Parks.

Public Works Accomplishments
This Administration is particularly proud that we are building the Municipal Services Garage with a federal Public Works Grant, secured through lobbying efforts in Washington, D.C. The more than $2,000,000 was provided by the Public Works Bill signed by President Carter in May, 1977, with Mayor Mowrer present at the ceremony.

Major capital projects accomplished during this year, with Public Works Department head George Perhac at the helm, included the reconstruction of West Lehigh Street, East Market Street, and Franklin Street; construction of East Boulevard and the Municipal Golf Course parking lot, the installation of the sanitary sewer on North Main Street and City-wide street overlays. Design work was completed for covering the open reservoir on the southside. On Creek Road, the department installed 2,500 feet of water main to solve well-water problems. Bethlehem sent much-needed manpower assistance to Johnstown after its disastrous flood.

Community Development Projects
With Franklin Gaugler as Director, restoration proposals for

the Sun Inn and the Grist Mill, and preparations for Main Street were completed. The inspection division approved new building construction estimated at $24,000,000.

Crime Reduced by Team Police

The Bethlehem Police Department, directed by Commissioner H. Robert Galle, completed another year of Team Police operations. We have reduced crime by 21.7%, which means that in 1977 Bethlehem has had its lowest level of major crimes in the past decade. The City has expanded the Crime Prevention program with concentration on premise security surveys, Project Theft-Guard, and the CHEC-MATE Program, a newly instituted program where citizens may report crime anonymously through a specially assigned number. The Crime Prevention Unit also assisted the Junior League of the Lehigh Valley with a comprehensive Crime Program in the public schools.

Fire Department Goals Achieved

The Bethlehem Fire Department, under the direction of commissioner Joseph Trilli, began a highly successful program of home-fire prevention inspections, and achieved the goal of inspecting 500 homes. The reactions of Bethlehem citizens have been very positive.

The department's in-service and pre-fire planning programs have been increased by 30%, and most of the commercial, industrial, and educational buildings in the city have been inspected. False alarms have dropped to a point where they are no longer a serious problem.

Administration Department Makes Strides

The Department of Administration, under the direction of Erma Aubert, conducted public auctions of 16 parcels of real estate, resulting in revenues of $440,225, and another auction of miscellaneous items which earned $4,855 for the city treasury. This Department also acted as coordinator of the city's Manpower Program, which includes 58 employees. Personnel completed the city's Affirmative Action Program, and worked to decrease interest costs to the City by refunding the 1975 bond issue for construction of the Sewage Treatment Plant Expansion.

Tourism Proposal for the City of Bethlehem
by Gordon B. Mowrer, Mayor
September, 1987
(Reprinted in its entirety)

Tourism in Bethlehem has reached a crossroads. During Christmas and Musikfest, our City is filled to capacity with people. Yet attracting a significant year-round flow of visitors to our community is still only a hope. Certainly, there are "bright stars" throughout the year, quality events staged by dedicated people, that have put Bethlehem "on the map." But I envision a more identifiable Bethlehem . . . a place in the sun . . . and under the star. I say: let's get tourism in gear during all 12 months of the year.

Bethlehem is in a unique position that allows it to capitalize on its year-round potential to attract visitors. We have a City that is at once steeped in the past, and poised for tomorrow. With the courage to think big, but the sensitivity to respect Bethlehem's dignified way of life, we can make Bethlehem "the place to be" all year round.

My addressing the question of year-round tourism was encouraged by the Bethlehem Area Chamber of Commerce through its president, Robert J. Kopecek. In February, Dr. Kopecek sent me a letter that stated the Chamber was "not prepared to finance the expansion of tourism that is needed to realize the potential of the community." The Chamber has done an outstanding job with the present tourism situation. Yet the candor of Dr. Kopecek's comments leads me to propose a new plan of action to attract visitors – a plan that encompasses everyone in Bethlehem.

It is my recommendation that we form an Authority to develop year-round tourism. An Authority would have both the financial teeth to pull in the tourist dollar, and the sensitivity to Bethlehem's pride that would keep a visitors program enjoyable and tasteful. The purpose of this group would not be to interfere in the operations of events such as Musikfest, or the Bach Festival. Instead, such an Authority would lead Bethlehem down the path of developing a dynamic and exciting presentation of the "Bethlehem Experience." I ask all of you today to be a part of breathing new life into our City. Let us provide the courage and vision it will take to make Bethlehem's star shine brighter.

Some of the advantages of creating an Authority are:

1. An Authority can have one major purpose, i.e. promoting tourism. Its efforts are not fractionated as are those of a department in City government.

2. Authorities are one step removed from the operation of City government.

3. Property can be bought, sold, owned and managed by an Authority.

4. An Authority can use bond financing to raise its own revenue.

5. Tax deductible contributions from the private sector can be accepted by an authority, which qualifies for the appropriate tax deduction.

6. A tourism Authority may have some taxation power (within a "tourism district," etc.)

The Authority

There are four major features of an Authority which would seem crucial to its success:

1. Efforts to draw people to Bethlehem would be

united within this Authority, including the responsibility for Christmas tourism, which now rests with the Chamber of Commerce. The Authority would be an umbrella organization for tourism. To allow efforts at increasing the number of visitors to Bethlehem to be fragmented is really self-defeating. A truly serious attempt to bring a constant flow of people to Bethlehem must be a consolidated effort.

The hope in forming an Authority to develop a visitors program is that those who are presently involved in overseeing tourism development in Bethlehem (Chamber of Commerce staff and volunteers, as well as others) could be utilized within the Authority.

2. The Authority must have the financial resources to implement ambitious plans. Its executive director should be an eminently capable individual, with experience in the field, a vision of how to attract people to Bethlehem, and an ability to get the job done. Both public and private funds should support the Authority. I propose that Bethlehem City Council commit fifty thousand dollars per year for the next five years to the Authority's efforts. This sum would be in addition to the ten thousand dollars presently given to the Lehigh Valley Convention and Visitors Bureau.

3. The Authority's charter should be for a period of time long enough to allow it to succeed, yet limited in a way that allows the Mayor, City Council, and the community to evaluate its effectiveness and determine whether to extend its charter. It should operate on the basis of one and five year plans with specific, measurable objectives.

It would seem that a natural period of time for such an evaluation would be in early 1992, after the 1991 celebration of Bethlehem's 250th Anniversary. The Authority's five year plan would call for it to plan and implement a year of celebration in 1991, in honor of Bethlehem's birthday. In 1992, the Authority's performance would be evaluated according to its progress in building year-round tourism, and its success in staging the 250th celebration.

During the five year period, I suggest that we explore with Lehigh Valley Bank the possibility of using the D. Patrick Robinson Center as a Visitors Center. Its successful use during last year's Christmas season indicates that the location and layout of the facilities will be suitable for this interim period. In 1992, if it is decided to extend the charter of the Authority, action could be taken on building a Visitors Center more along the lines of that described in the Schwarz/Parker report. Building a new Visitors Center now does not seem prudent. Let us take the next five years to determine the scope of the visitors program that will be developed here. We do not need a Visitors Center void of visitors.

4. The Authority would also have the responsibility of catalyzing the creation of supportive resources such as public restrooms, parking, etc. This infrastructure is crucial to Bethlehem's creating and maintaining a significant flow of visitors.

In my judgement, creating this Authority is the best course of action for tourism development. However, there are other options which can be taken.

Other Options

1. Maintain or increase the amount of funds given to the Chamber of Commerce to run tourism in Bethlehem.

If we are determined to maintain our present status, the Chamber would then continue to develop and operate tourism in Bethlehem. City Council might choose to increase the level of funding given towards the Chamber's efforts. This would enable the Chamber's Tourism Committee to increase the levels of advertising and promotion it presently utilizes.

2. The Lehigh Valley Convention and Visitors Bureau could be made responsible for all of tourism in Bethlehem. This would include the creation and development of new programs in addition to their present roles of promotion and marketing.

Promotion of the Valley as a whole is important, and will remain so regardless of whether a tourism Authority is created. There would be advantages to putting all our efforts at increasing tourism into this Valley-wide tourism organization. The visitors package that could be developed would encompass two counties, rather than just one city. There would be a greater ability on the part of the Lehigh Valley Convention and Visitors Bureau to package Bethlehem's activities and tours with other attractions throughout Lehigh and Northampton Counties.

3. A separate bureau for tourism could be established at City Hall which would report directly to the Mayor. This bureau then would be responsible for the development of tourism in Bethlehem.

4. The Collegium could be given the responsibility for developing all of tourism in Bethlehem (as suggested in the Schwarz/Parker report.)

Why Promote More Tourism?

There are two major reasons why an effort to fulfill our potential as a visitors site should be pursued.

1. Community Pride.

A visitors program that successfully displays Bethlehem's proud heritage will create community pride, and a greater propensity for involvement by our citizens. This fact has been well documented by the support Musikfest has received.

2. Economic Development.

Tourism could be financially lucrative for Bethlehem. Existing merchants will benefit from, and new entrepreneurs will be drawn by a successful effort to attract visitors to our City. In many ways, the commercial sections of downtown Bethlehem have already become oriented towards the needs of visitors. The relatively new eating establishments and boutiques in this area are taking advantage of Bethlehem's unique atmosphere. Future projects will add to this already encouraging situation. The proposed Goodman Reading Passenger Terminal Restoration will be an extremely attractive place to visit. This project is especially significant because of its location on Third Street, which would serve to tie the North and South Sides together in an effort to attract visitors. The Quality Suites Hotel proposed for Third and Brodhead Streets is another South Side project that will be an exciting addition to Bethlehem's facilities. Certainly, development of the Broad and Main Streets lot will also greatly help to commercially attract visitors.

The Authority could help build upon this exciting commercial base. Cooperating with the other economic interests in the community would allow the Authority to develop and implement programs in which the merchants would "help and be helped." By keeping track of available retail space, and actively seeking to attract new merchants to Bethlehem, the Authority could enable further commercial growth in the downtown. The economic renewal that such efforts could bring about is a significant reason why an Authority should be created to encourage year-round tourism.

A visitors program built around the five points of the Bethlehem Star will be in harmony with our community, thus enabling us to teach and share with others those things of which Bethlehem is most proud.

Building on the Five Points of the Star

Industry

Industry has always been an important part of our community. The Waterworks contain the first pumping water system ever built in the American colonies. The Grist Mill and Tannery are the other integral parts of an 18th Century Industrial complex that is the forerunner of a long line of industrial innovations that took place in Bethlehem. Historic Bethlehem, Inc. has done an outstanding job of restoring these facilities and utilizing them to educate residents and visitors about our City's past.

In 1854, Bethlehem Iron Works was founded. As this organization became Bethlehem Steel (at the turn of the century) the city of Bethlehem was changing and growing, leaving behind its status as a semi-rural town, and becoming a significant industrial City. The canal and railroad industries became important along with the Steel, and all served to make Bethlehem a nationally significant community. The creation of a Steel/Industrial Production Museum that would tell about this important part of Bethlehem's history has long been suggested. The Authority would be instrumental in bringing this proposal to reality. It would include exhibits, programs, and tours that would bring home to people the hot, heavy, dangerous work that has helped make Bethlehem what it is today.

The history of industry in Bethlehem does not end at the turn of the century. The Lehigh Valley Industrial Park continued the Bethlehem tradition of having a visionary and innovative approach to commercial success. Organizations such as the Ben Franklin Program operated under the State Department of Commerce prepare Bethlehem for the 21st Century, by helping small businesses to survive in a more competitive and technical marketplace. Business people from around the world have been attracted to our city because of these organizations.

It is in this same tradition of creativity and innovation that increased support for the tourism industry should be considered. In many ways, the business of attracting visitors is custom made for our City. By showcasing the accomplishments of those who came before us, and making people aware of the quality of our community today, Bethlehem can benefit greatly. Tourism, the second largest industry in Pennsylvania, could play a significant role in Bethlehem's social and economic life.

Education

Bethlehem's tradition of educational excellence is also a well known feature of our city. The Moravians commitment to education is obvious here, with Moravian College and Moravian Academy tracing their origins back to 1742. Moreover, the first women's school founded in the original thirteen colonies, the Moravian Seminary for Girls, was located here. Lehigh University is a nationally prominent school with an impressive history of academic excellence. Other educational institutions that have enriched our city are Moravian Theological Seminary and Northampton

County Area Community College. These schools play a direct and important role in tourism. They attract visitors from throughout the world to attend conferences and symposiums on many different topics. A substantial number of parents spend time in Bethlehem during visits with their children who attend these institutions. In addition, our city has a fine public and parochial school system, which help to make up the educational heritage of Bethlehem.

In its own way, Bethlehem's tourism program must stay true to this commitment to education. The educational aspect of a visitors program is extremely important. It is crucial that the role of the non-profit organizations as historical educators be encouraged and supported by the Authority. "Bringing history alive" by having colonial crafts produced in the refurbished colonial buildings has often been suggested as a way to attract and educate a great number of people about Bethlehem's history. The restoration and use of the 1749 Pottery should be a part of such an endeavor. The Authority could aid Historic Bethlehem, Inc. in obtaining the funds necessary to complete such a project. In addition, a cooperative effort with Moravian College could result in faculty and students from the art department actually making pottery in the original building. The Burnside Plantation is another historical landmark that should be utilized in making history "come alive" in Bethlehem.

Mr. Robert Snyder has made a number of suggestions concerning types of tours and programs that could be implemented during the summer months. Just one example is an "Architectural Walking Tour of Church Street." This tour would be led by a guide, who would point out the 200+ years of architectural development that can be seen on Church Street alone. Other potential programs are:

"Bethlehem and the Revolutionary War"
"Two Centuries of Decorative Art"
"Indians and Bethlehem"
"A Walk with General Washington " (guided tour through the Sun Inn, Brethren's House, Waterworks, and Tannery – all of which Washington visited).

(For a complete list, refer to the Bethlehem Visitors Collegium Proposal for a "Typical Summer Schedule," and to their "Packaging Sample – Hotel Bethlehem.")

Music

Certainly, the musical heritage of Bethlehem is well known and has been built upon successfully by the Bach Festival and programs of Moravian music. The Municipal Band, as well as our national award-winning high school bands, could be better shown off if more community concerts were staged in the City's bandshells. Lehigh University's Stabler Arena regularly draws a significant number of people for concerts. Stabler's capability of seating large numbers of people is another resource that could be taken greater advantage of by the Authority. The excitement of Musikfest speaks for itself. Bethlehem's citizens share with their friends and relatives a variety of musical offerings during the nine day festival.

Religion

Bethlehem has a long and diverse religious history, reflecting the many different people who have made up our community over the years. People of all faiths and practices – Christians and Jews, Protestants and Catholics – have added to the character of the City. The Moravian Church has had a most significant impact on our community. Special and unique services are held not only at Christmas but at Eastertime as well. Today there are numerous Moravian music festivals that are held where the rich musical heritage of the church is sustained and shared. The many Catholic ethnic churches on the South Side are a testimony to the diversity of our people, with masses being given in Portuguese, Spanish, Hungarian, Polish, Windish, Czechoslovakian, among others.

Amidst all this diversity, since Bethlehem was first named on Christmas Eve 1741, the Christmas story has played an integral part in Community life. The Star and the Christmas lights of the holiday season create a special atmosphere in which the putz and vespers services are the focus of attention. Christmas will always play a large role in tourism here. Yet a year-round visitors program will work to illustrate the rich diversity of religious beliefs and practices visible in Bethlehem.

Recreation

Bethlehem has always recognized the importance of recreation. Today we boast of over 1,000 acres of parkland that make possible many activities for both residents and visitors. Fishing, softball, baseball, and soccer are all enjoyed on public property. Both nine and eighteen-hole municipal golf courses are available. The quality of Sand Island's tennis courts is another attractive recreational feature of Bethlehem. Canoeing and jogging on the Lehigh Canal are pleasures that cannot be duplicated in most communities. All of these activities are available in the same community where one can enjoy a walk through Monocacy Park with its beautiful waterfall, the Rose Garden with its flowers in full bloom and the City Center with its Serenity Garden and Sculpture Garden.

In addition to the traditional recreational offerings, the Pennsylvania Playhouse and the soon to be completed Touchstone Theatre offer unique opportunities for entertainment. With all of these possibilities for enjoyment already in existence, Bethlehem has a solid recreational base upon which an Authority could build year-round tourism.

Conclusion

By stimulating discussion, interaction, and perhaps even controversy, it is my desire that this report will aid the effort to bring year-round tourism to Bethlehem. In my opinion, a tourism Authority is the best way to make the hope of year-round tourism become a reality. In the 1988 budget, I will propose to City Council that $50,000 be allocated for the establishment of such an Authority. I encourage City Council and the new Mayor to support this program for the next five years.

Such an effort to increase tourism builds on Bethlehem's traditional open door policy for visitors. Bethlehem has opened its doors to visitors such as Lafayette, Pulaski, George Washington, Benjamin Franklin, and even Mark Twain, and a great many others as well. It seems only natural that we continue in this tradition of allowing visitors to share in our past, our present, and our future. A tourism Authority will certainly face many challenges and hurdles in the path toward success, but the time has come for decisiveness and forward motion. In attaining the ultimate goal of year-round tourism in Bethlehem, the tourism Authority has the best chance to succeed.

Index